Ice Cream Travel Guide

Ice Cream
Travel Guide

Jennifer Ng

Photography and book design by Jennifer Ng.

First published 2016, Think-Ng Media

Typeset in **Montserrat** and Josefin Slab

ISBN-10: 0-9976086-0-9
ISBN-13: 978-0-9976086-0-1

For TaiChE, the cone to my scoop

Contents

Prologue   9

San Francisco   14

   Bacetti   18

   Smitten   22

   Mr. and Mrs. Miscellaneous   27

   Mitchell's   31

   Recipe: Eucalyptus Ice Cream   36

Seattle   37

   Parfait Ice Cream   42

   Bluebird Microcreamery   47

   Half Pint Ice Cream   52

   Mora Iced Creamery   56

   Recipe: Roasted Strawberry and Carmelized Banana Ice   62
   Cream

Los Angeles   64

   Mashti Malone's   68

   Coolhaus   73

   KindKreme   78

   Kiwi Lime Sorbet   83

Columbus and Around   84

   Vienna Ice   90

   Young's Jersey Dairy   94

   Recipe: Goat Cheese Ice Cream with Carmelized Figs and   100
   Candied Bacon

Snowville Creamery: 102
A Visit to a Dairy Plant

New York City — 110

Victory Garden — 114

The Original Chinatown Ice Cream Factory — 119

Van Leeuwen — 124

Recipe: Celery Ice Cream with Peanut Butter Swirl and Rum-Soaked Raisins — 130

Philadelphia and Around — 132

Franklin Fountain — 136

Bassetts Ice Cream — 142

Woodside Farm Creamery — 147

Recipe: Spiced Apple Ice Cream with Caramel Swirl — 152

Vancouver — 154

Bella Gelateria — 158

La Casa Gelato — 163

Earnest Ice Cream — 168

Recipe: Roasted Peach Sorbet — 173

Taipei and Around — 174

Snow King (雪王) — 180

Recipe: Pur-Erh Ice Cream — 186

Shaved Ice in Asia — 187

Manila — 192

Sebastian's Ice Cream — 196

Carmen's Best — 201

Merry Moo — 206

Recipe: Passion Fruit and Mango Ice Cream — 211

Buenos Aires — 212

Heladeria Fratello — 218

Heladeria Cadore — 223

Recipe: Dulce de Leche Granizado Ice Cream — 228

Istanbul 230

Girandola Dondurma 234

Recipe: Watermelon Mint Sorbet 244

Visiting the Carpigiani Gelato University and Museum 245

Bologna 252

Gelateria Sole Luna 256

La Sorbetteria Castiglione 261

Recipe: Blood Orange Sorbet with Candied Peels 268

Rome 270

Il Gelato di Claudio Torce 276

Fior di Luna 282

Gelateria di Gracchi 288

Recipe: Raspberry Lemon Sorbet 293

Sicily: Finding the Origin of Ice Cream on a Southern Italian Island 294

Epilogue 303

Acknowledgements 310

About the Author 314

Prologue

It all started with something cold.

Over four thousand years ago, valley civilizations, enveloped by humidity, gazed at snow-capped mountains. There, they saw the memories of past winters. Men climbed the mountains, packed up the snow, and lugged it back to their villages to be stored. Besides cold food storage, the snow was mixed with fruit, wine, or honey. This was the first flavored ice that evolved to today's sorbets and granitas. The world experienced the early origins of a cold dessert.

But we don't know how ice cream exactly originated. I am talking about the creamy mixture of milk, cream, and sugar. Maybe a housewife discovered that adding salt to the snow lowered its freezing point; maybe there was a curious child who kicked around a canister of custard until it turned into ice cream. Did ice cream evolve from the popular cooled fruit drinks of the time named *sharbat*? Or from

Emperor Nero, who sent his servants up volcanic Mt. Etna in Sicily to gather ice for cold desserts? Was it the Chinese, who froze a mixture of ground rice and milk in snow? Did it come from Marco Polo, who adapted the Chinese recipe to European tastes? No other food has had such mysterious origins as ice cream.

My own story, like that of many ice cream lovers, started in childhood and got renewed when I walked into my first artisanal ice cream shop. I could begin by regaling you with stories of how my dad always served ice cream to my sister and me after dinner. It was a small scoop of either mint chocolate chip or strawberry ice cream, served in a small blue ceramic bowl. After I finished eating what was in my bowl, I dipped my finger into my sister's bowl to find more rewards. Or, I could tell you about how, like many twenty-somethings, I filled my freezer with supermarket brand ice cream. Then, in frustration, celebration, or heartbreak, I dug a spoon into the creamy indulgence and let the dessert fill me up with delight.

That ice cream could hardly be called artisanal. The strawberry ice cream was bright pink and lacked strawberry chunks. In other words, my childhood ice cream (and the ice cream I afforded as a college student) was definitely industrial—made, in a large factory, and dyed bright colors to draw attention.

The story resumed during a summer evening in Pennsylvania, when I was in my early twenties. Having moved hundreds of miles away from my hometown, I thirsted for new experiences. The smell of freshly made waffle cones drew me into Dave & Andy's, a local ice cream shop on a tree-filled neighborhood street. Former milk jugs served as seats. Brightly colored walls showcased achievements. One clipping declared Dave & Andy's as one of the top five ice cream shops in the area. Having grown up in suburban America (where ice cream came from grocery stores), I had never experienced homemade ice cream that was made in small batches. Family-owned shops were rarely on my radar; Cold Stone Creamery and Baskin Robbins were the most popular ice cream shops. I pressed my nose against the ice cream display case, impressed with the array of flavors and scents.

The generous scooper who worked there offered samples of ice cream flavors: from white chocolate cinnamon habañero, to strawberry, to birthday cake (my adventurous choice at the time). He dropped a red M&M into the waffle cone to prevent unwanted drips from the bottom. Then he laid a scoop of ice cream on top. With just one lick, a new era began for me. It was an era full of repeated visits to this local shop, of drives just to have a scoop of ice cream that was located fifty miles away, and of international trips that were planned around finding the best local ice cream.

In Boston, my friends laughed when I insisted on visiting the famous ice cream shops, J.P. Licks and Toscanini's. In New York, my sister sighed, but smiled as I dragged her from a classic Brooklyn Creamery to a popular gelato shop in the East Village.

After moving back to California, my love of good food became a full-blown obsession. With the sudden surge of ice cream shops opening in San Francisco, I had found a home for myself. As if magnetized, I found myself in front of local ice cream shops like Bi-Rite Creamery, Humphry Slocombe, and Mitchell's Ice Cream. In San Francisco, I became more familiar with the operation of small ice cream shops, and especially with my growing awareness of wanting to know more about our food's origins.

Yet, why wasn't there a guide to ice cream around the world? I saw guides to beer, guides to wine, and guides to cheese. What about those of us who want something else? Something sweet, refreshing, and cold? I had read lists that slapped together ten names of random global ice cream shops. Occasionally, I would find the name of an ice cream shop in a travel book, buried at the bottom of the dining section. Truth be told, there is no worldwide guide to ice cream.

The one defining characteristic of ice cream is: it melts. Perhaps that's the best part of it—we are left with a soft, syrupy mess that cools our tongues and makes our fingers sticky. The melting of ice cream leads us to an obvious, but important, conclusion: ice cream just doesn't travel well. Unlike a bottle of wine that can easily travel, ice cream is never quite the same once it travels 100 miles. Sure, a kiwi grown in Italy can be eaten in New York City, or an unripe mango plucked from a tree in the Philippines can be mixed with yogurt in the United Kingdom. But ice cream? Unless it is distributed locally, great quality ice cream cannot survive the changing temperatures during travel. It's simply best when it's fresh.

Dessert lovers ask me the difference between ice cream and gelato. It is nearly the same, because gelato and ice cream are nearly interchangeable. Yes, gelato is held a bit warmer and has less fat. But at its core, it's the same. It is a cold dessert, and I must learn more.

So began the one year of traveling to learn about ice cream around the world. Starting in San Francisco, I made my way across the United States. Then I ventured abroad to Asia, South America, and Europe. By the year's end, I had met with more than sixty ice cream shop owners and conversed with them in more than five different languages. During that year I chatted with ice cream bloggers, I flew over 50,322 miles in coach, I stayed at a dairy farm and many private homes, and I licked over a hundred pounds of ice cream!

What follows is a travel guide to ice cream in multiple countries. I have highlighted ice cream destinations and profiled selected shops. Now, go forth and lick some ice cream!

Note: Each city map indicates the ice cream shops that I have personally visited for the purposes of this book. Those indicated with a ⭐ are profiled in this book. Confirm the listed address of ice cream shop by visiting their website.

1

San Francisco

"The coldest winter I ever experienced was a summer in San Francisco."
- Unknown

Was it Mark Twain who said that? Was it a native San Franciscan? Whatever the case, San Francisco is not just any California city.

The steep hills give San Francisco unique micro-climates—sunny in the west and chilly in the east. From downtown to the outlying areas, the fog melts like a giant bowl of ice cream. New residents quickly learn two things: be prepared for any change of the weather, and ice cream is perfect any day of the year.

Bounded by the world-renowned University of California, Berkeley and Stanford, San Francisco embodies a liberal population tempered by the history of immigrants from all over the world. The city is a foodie paradise where the tech culture reigns. To the south of the city, Silicon Valley and the likes of HP and Oracle fuel the economy and job market. To the northeast of the city, the heart of the California wine industry in the Napa Valley attracts the foodies and tourists.

Eating in the city is all about the local ingredients and innovation. Lush organic farms rush to sell at the city farmers markets—fresh peaches for $4 a pound and peppers for $1 each. Restaurants like Slanted Door, Delfina, and others involved in the Slow Food movement dominate. Immortalized by Anthony Bourdain at *That's It Market*, the *torta cubana* can be found in many variations. Food trucks and carts like the Creme Brulee cart and others continue the food revolution in low-cost quality gourmet food.

This is my hometown and the starting point of our journey to discover the world's take on ice cream.

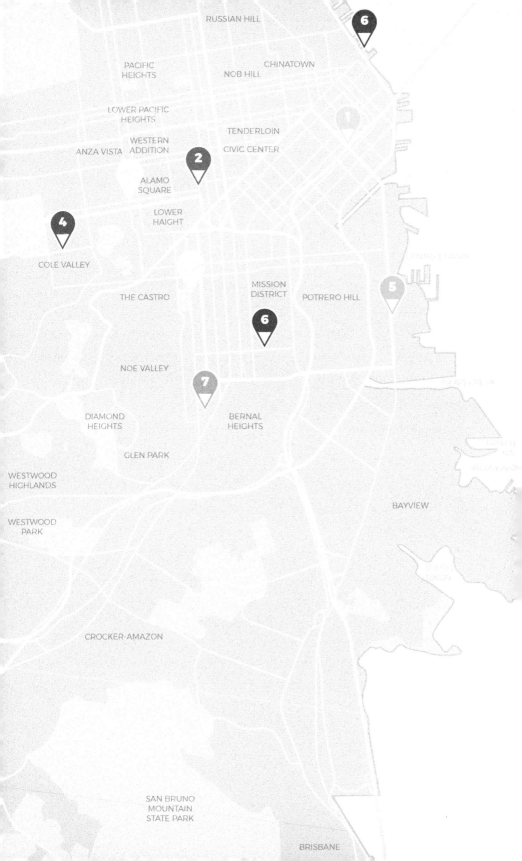

Frozen Kuhsterd

frozenkuhsterd.com

Food truck roving location
and hours

Bacetti

bacetti.com

Inside Chantal Guillon

1309 Howard St

   (415) 512-1020

Smitten

smittenicecream.com

432 Octavia St #1A

   (415) 863-1518

Bi-Rite Creamery

biritecreamery.com

3692 18th St

   (415) 626-5600

550 Divisadero St

   (415) 551-7900

Ice Cream Bar

theicecreambarsf.com

815 Cole St

   (415) 742-4932

Mr. and Mrs. Miscellaneous

mrandmrsmiscellaneous.com

699 22nd St

   (415) 970-0750

Humphry Slocombe

humphryslocombe.com

(415) 550-6971

2790 Harrison St

1 Ferry Building

Mitchell's

mitchellsicecream.com

688 San Jose Ave

   (415) 648-2300

Bacetti

Bacetti was founded by Franco-Italian siblings who wanted to bring Italian cuisine to San Francisco. Serving gelato bites dipped in chocolate, flavors range from the Italian favorite pine nut to classic vanilla. Today, one can also find another French sweet delight, hand-crafted macarons, alongside the bacetti.

bacetti.com

Inside Chantal Guillon

1309 Howard St

(415) 512-1020

In mid-2010 on the busy thoroughfare on Harrison Street, I noticed a two-floor building, painted with bold Helvetica letters and alternating blue and cream diamonds. The building broke the modicum of the concrete environment, dedicated to startups. My eyes caught the words "ice cream", "Bacetti", and "Coming soon." My heart was stolen.

On a brown garage door, white block letters declare, "No Parking, people are waiting for their bacetti!" Through the front door, a display case contains chocolate-dipped gelato in finger-sized packages—the colored diamonds of the wrapper reflecting its flavor. The chocolate mousse flavors are deep brown. Vanilla is sky blue. Wrapped bacetti with green diamonds signifies mint combining mint paste and chocolate. Behind the display case, a corridor opens to the production. Like a line of drying laundry, a hanging wire carries gelato bites dipped in melted chocolate. Flowing chilled air solidifies the chocolate. With a swift motion, an employee grasps an individual bacetti and wraps it in the signature foil wrapper, printed with colored diamonds.

When I worked nearby, Bacetti remained omnipresent—a dessert within steps. As an office treat, I picked up a freezer bag, filled with over fifty pieces of bacetti and dry ice. Back in the office, coworkers welcomed the prized bag as a welcomed reprieve from computer work. We unwrapped the pieces and bit into them, letting the chocolate melt into the creamy gelato. Roasted pine nuts added a nutty layer. Vanilla surprised the timid with its intense flavor. Chocolate mousse wove through chocolate gelato for a chocolate delight. Salted caramel mixed savory and sweet notes. Colored white, the mint bacetti recalled memories of homegrown garden mint plants. The orange zest bacetti had bits of orange peel sprinkled through the gelato.

The siblings Alexandra and Cedric Di Donato founded Bacetti. Hailing from Europe, they grew up surrounded by a Franco-Italian culture. When their parents separated, they went to different countries.

Alexandra traveled to France with their mother, who worked at high-end restaurants. Cedric stayed in Italy with their father, who did interior design. They eventually lived in the same city in Italy.

Like many Italians, Alexandra established a distinct routine. At 11 AM, Alexandra would have white pasta. Then somewhere between 1 and 2 PM, she visited a local trattoria. Afterwards, she had gelato or a frozen yogurt. If she was with her brother, after work, they headed downtown to the plaza to have coffee, ice cream, and cigarettes with their friends. Usually, in that order.

Drawn by opportunity in the United States, the siblings arrived to expand their father's interior design business in Los Angeles. The design included textiles, ceramics, and mosaics, some from San Francisco. Within a few years, the interior design business closed due to a departing partner. "Our luggage was here," Cedric says. "Staying here [in the United States] was an easy choice."

At cafes in Italy, a gelato bite dipped in chocolate is served with coffee as complimentary refreshment. Inspired by the colors and patterns in the city, the siblings decided to introduce the refreshment to San Francisco. Taking almost a year to put everything together, the siblings founded Bacetti in 2009. Cedric describes, "We figured we'd introduce a new fusion of a coffee shop with the magic of a handmade bite."

"In San Francisco, everybody loves coffee," Alexandra adds. "They also love ice cream even if it's cold. We wanted to put a Franco-Italian spin on that."

Cedric exclaims, "Let's give people the ice cream and coffee. Bacetti is just a little square. Easy to enjoy even in the frozen weather."

The siblings create all flavors while balancing European and American preferences. "Eventually, we will serve affogato—coffee over ice cream," Cedric says. "And it doesn't have to be over the bacetti."

Their signature flavor? As children, they stumbled across pinecones. Breaking the shell to the nuts required strength. Once opened, they brought the results to their aunt to incorporate into recipes. Inspired by the popularity of pine nuts, the pine nut embodies much of the philosophy of Bacetti. The nuts add a layer to the bacetti, offering a distinctive European flavor. "You can tell when it's natural pine nuts," Alexandra says. "They are slightly roasted in our bacetti."

"We believe that it's good to sell something you like," Cedric says. "These are things that we loved."

Bacetti sells from their storefront and partners with local businesses like restaurants. A single piece can be purchased. Bacetti also offers a set of six pieces perfect for a family. Special orders, like my office treat, are common. The square is not too big and not too small. One sibling chirps, "Each bacetti has only 60 calories and 4 grams of sugar."

When I visit Bacetti, Alexandra or Cedric mans the front. Entranced visitors ask about the design and the food. "Everyone wants to know the people behind Bacetti," Cedric says.

Bacetti thrives, and the siblings love being here. They observe that American business invites collaboration rather than competition. "Here in the United States, Americans smile and laugh," Alexandra says. "They have open minds. Italians are difficult. Products are traditional."

"In Europe, if the products have a well-known name, they trust it," Cedric adds. "It would be hard to open up Bacetti in Europe."

"People are sad in Paris," Alexandra says and shakes her head. "There is a mentality that everything is trouble. The French are stressed. Americans are not scared to share skills and ideas. That's what works."

Smitten

Smitten combines the old and the new in its ice cream, by using locally sourced ingredients and liquid nitrogen. The ice cream is served out of a former shipping container next to a popular small park in Hayes Valley neighborhood.

smittenicecream.com

432 Octavia St #1A

(415) 863-1518

A tree-lined boulevard leads to Patricia's Green, a neighborhood park created due to the efforts of neighborhood activists who successfully reclaimed the freeway thoroughfare damaged in the 1989 Loma Prieta earthquake. Today, the park serves as the hub of the renewed neighborhood. Children and adults clamber through a dome playground structure and gaze at art installations from the Burning Man festival.

Smitten Ice Cream sits at the corner of Octavia Street and Linden Street. Linden Street is a small alley filled with foodies spilling out from a beer garden and coffee stands. The exterior of Smitten Ice Cream is painted stainless steel, and its bulk hints at its former life as a shipping container transporting goods around the world. Next to the ordering window, warm wood with red lettering beckons patrons to look at the chalkboard of flavors. Four flavors display daily. One flavor changes seasonally—honey nectarine in the summer and maple brown sugar squash in the fall. Each flavor shows its array of ingredients as paper-like cutouts. Extracts, artificial flavors, and colors are absent. Vanilla ice cream, one of the mainstays, is represented as a bottle of milk with a cow, a bag of sugar, vanilla beans, a salt shaker, and an egg.

Mixing the old and new world is the goal of Smitten. Ice cream lovers are dazzled by the floating clouds from the liquid nitrogen ice cream machines. The ice cream is best eaten immediately after it is made. Every customer is given the 100% Smitten satisfaction guarantee: If they're not happy, bring it back.

Robyn Sue Fisher walks out from a side door of Smitten. Her dark hair is tied back. She just tested a batch of vanilla crème fraiche. Mint now steeps in an ice cream base, a mixture of milk, cream, and sugar. Whole ingredients from local sources have arrived in the kitchen. Robyn Lyn, another innovator with the same name and a former pastry chef, works furiously as the *Chef de Brrr* coming up with new flavors.

Sitting on a concrete bench, Robyn Sue glances at Smitten. Thoughts run through her mind—upcoming Smitten events, new flavors to test and experiment, and managing her crew. What about an ice cream flavor with butternut squash and maple? Which flavor will sell best?

As a self-proclaimed ice cream fanatic, Robyn Sue visited ice cream shops as a child. Growing up outside Boston, Herell's Ice Cream and Christina's were common stops. Her mother believed that Robyn had

two stomachs—one for ice cream and another for everything else. They drove to find ice cream, sometimes up to forty minutes or more. "It was my happy thing," Robyn Sue says. "It was a whole adventure."

After finishing a graduate degree in product design and entrepreneurship, Robyn Sue explored how ice cream could be better. In recent decades, chemicals added to ice cream helped make it creamier and last longer. She didn't want any part of that. "Ice cream is moving away from the cow," she tells me.

Back in San Francisco, she noticed how flavors were seasonal and high quality in local ice cream shops. Yet, how could she stand out among them? What could she do to bring back original ice cream? What could she do to create adventure and quality? It was a quandary. "Old and new," she recalls her thinking. "I wanted to bring ice cream back in time."

Liquid nitrogen was her solution. The liquid nitrogen helped make the ice crystals smaller and didn't allow air to be trapped, resulting in a rich and dense mixture within seconds. It was 50% denser than traditional ice cream and unlike anything else on the market. She was thrilled. How to mix it though? A bowl and whisk seemed fine for small batches and a KitchenAid stand mixer for bigger ones. However, Robyn Sue had other plans.

Drawing from her life savings, she built a prototype that allowed for large scale churning of her liquid nitrogen ice cream. Soliciting her network for names, she named the machine Kelvin after the thermodynamic temperature scale. Later due to name confusion, the name was changed to Brrr. After spending two years perfecting the machine in her parents' backyard and using everyone she knew as willing guinea pigs, Robyn Sue Fisher launched Smitten on a Radio Flyer wagon in a San Francisco park. Pulling Brrr around this way drew people to her. The simplicity and old-fashioned quality of ice cream turned them into fans.

With the unexpected success, she moved to a permanent location within a former shipping container. Her colleagues come from San Francisco institutions and have added their culinary expertise to Smitten. Serving four flavors daily, ice cream lovers can enjoy ice cream at Patricia's Green across the street or pair it with a meal from food trucks during weekly Off the Grid events.

More locations have opened in the Bay Area, all retaining the old and new look, feel, and traditions of the original. Brrr is in its second iteration, which will not be its last. Even at a premium, customers clamor for more. Once they order a flavor, they watch it created at one of four stations, each representing a flavor. A Brrrista pours the ice cream base into Brrr and presses a button. The ice cream churns and a cloud of evaporating water flows out, creating a magical scene. The customer's name is called. A cup is given in the opening with a spoon ready for the dense ice cream to be eaten with each bite bursting with flavor.

"I can't ask for a better job," Robyn Sue says.

I have tried the liquid nitrogen approach at home. Finding a supplier, I obtained five liters of the volatile liquid nitrogen—volatile more for its rapid evaporation than its inherent danger. In a bowl with my ice cream base, I poured the liquid nitrogen while whisking with rapid and intense strokes. The liquid nitrogen lowered the temperature of the base quickly and with the churning, small crystals were formed. The resulting ice cream captured the ingredients—denser than the standard ice cream and highlighting the fresh strawberries from local markets.

Mr. and Mrs. Miscellaneous

Mr. and Mrs. Miscellaneous was conceived by a couple who worked as chefs. Located in the Dogpatch neighborhood, the couple serves a rotating list of ice cream flavors that complements their savory and sweet tastes.

mrandmrsmiscellaneous.com

699 22nd St

(415) 970-0750

"Ice cream is a canvas," Ian Flores begins. "It can be everything."

Ian Flores and his business partner, Ann Topacio, love simplicity. Ice cream was the answer. Originally pastry chefs at fine dining restaurants, they wanted a change of lifestyle as they started a new family together. What if they also interacted with the customers? Having trained at the country's top culinary schools, they knew the culinary network and artisanal food scene. They had worked at places such as Chez Panisse, Aqua, Cut, and Spago— all five-star fine dining restaurants that set a high bar for quality, locally-sourced ingredients.

Four months before expecting their first child, they found a space near their apartment in the Dogpatch neighborhood. Located a few blocks from a commuter train station, the neighborhood is busy during the week and quiets during the weekend. Once a warehouse district, the area is slowly gentrifying with cafes and condominiums.

Although the business is small—it's primarily the two of them running the shop, they work from six in the morning to ten at night to ensure its success. "We were dumb enough [to start a business]," Ian recalls.

But they are pleased with the success although they both need to work the front of the house and the back of the house. "It's different from cooking," Ian says. "It's a labor of love. We never compromise."

Ian admires Ann for her dexterity and determination in a male-dominant profession. In fact, the name Mr. and Mrs. Miscellaneous came out of that respect. They wanted whimsy and memorability. But most importantly, a name that represented equality—Ian and Ann are equal partners in the business.

"It's important that everyone knows that there is a woman too behind the scenes," he says. "It's not just me."

It is now February, and customers still pour into the shop. Ian sits across from me at one of the long black wooden tables that fill the tall airy space. Chocolate brown chairs surround the tables. A small water jug sits in the corner with triangle-shaped paper cups. Ian and Ann designed the shop together, carefully selecting tables and chairs to achieve their desired aesthetic.

"We put our heart and soul into it," Ian glances the space. "It feels like our house."

As they scoop, their tattooed arms move gracefully up and down into their freezer at counter height. The ice cream is not on display. It's kept at the ideal temperature in a top door cabinet. Daily rotating flavors are written in colored chalk and fill a large chalkboard.

As Ian speaks, every few sentences are punctuated with "That's crazy, man!" He recalls the dynamic of San Francisco ice cream shops — "we're all friends and everyone knows each other"—and the surprising opening day in May 2010—"it was so packed." Ian acknowledges the fans, "We're lucky that other people like what we do." He mentions a few buddies who came and hung out—Manny from SPQR, a well-respected restaurant, Jake Godby from Humphry Slocombe, an ice cream shop known for "wacky" flavors, and Liz from Brickmaiden Bread, a famous bakery located north of the city.

In work and in life, Ian and Ann are absolute complements. They met at a book signing, introduced by a colleague, Sherry Yard—the former executive pastry chef at Spago. Ian, with his love of savory, brings the deeper, intense flavors to the shop. He moves fast. He loves chocolate chip, peanut butter, and coffee. Ann, with a passion in baking and trained at the famous Culinary Institute of America in New York, experiments with flavors that are subtle and surprising. Beer and spice embody much of her creations like the flavor fig & brandy.

Ann loves the process of making bread. "I find it like watching paint dry," Ian chuckles.

I ask him what he considers the most important lesson he has learned so far in running his business.

"Having street cred is the most valuable thing," Ian says. "Any day could be our last. Remember what happened during the Fudgesicle Incident?"

Since the shop's inception, the menu has featured a chocolate-flavored popsicle which offered a diversion from the ice cream scoops. Until about late 2010, they called it a Fudgesicle. Unilever, the corporation that owns the Popsicle brand, threatened to sue Mr. and Mrs. Miscellaneous for an unofficial use of their trademark. Ian and Ann were nonplussed. In fact, they were impressed that a large corporation learned of their small business. Playing off the whimsical situation, they renamed the bar to "Trademark Bar."

As each bite melts on my tongue, the flavors meld, rise, and disappear into a sweet finish. The fruit-based flavors, which are rarely found on the menu, entice me the most. Regardless, I love their consistency in the ice cream texture. It is the same visit to visit. Ian and Ann make only what they like when they like. Though their flavors are familiar, sometimes a twist or two, guided by Ian and Ann's culinary knowledge, will make an appearance.

They know how to pair flavors. Ian suggests flavors like basil chip, pine nut & Parmesan, violet chip, and floral lemon. While Ian admires the young chefs who experiment, he doesn't go to their extremes. He and Ann believe that long-term quality rooted in tradition and long-established recipes will always survive ever-changing trends driven by impulsive experiments.

"We're happy being small and doing what we want," he says. "We don't want to be 'used to be good'."

Mitchell's

Mitchell's is one of the few remaining San Francisco ice cream shops from the 1950s, an era of soda fountains and ice cream parlors. Known for the ice cream flavors of mango and ube (purple yam), the ice cream shop has rapidly adapted to the changing residents in the neighborhood of the Mission.

mitchellsicecream.com

688 San Jose Ave

(415) 648-2300

To me, Mitchell's is a distinct personal memory, representing a moment in San Francisco. Despite growing up just over twenty miles outside the city, San Francisco was a rare destination. But in 2000, adventure beckoned my sister and me, when we were in our early twenties. Back then, digital wayfinding was in its infancy, so we relied on printed Yahoo maps to navigate the complex freeway interchanges to our destination. After squabbling over the intention of "drive straight onto the underpass" and "take the first exit on 280," we pulled up to the first friendly-looking building. Inside, employees assuaged our frustrations and offered ice cream as they helped us navigate the city. I don't remember what I ordered. Perhaps cookies 'n cream or butter pecan. For my sister, mint chocolate chip. With ice cream in our belly and directions clarified, we found our friend's house.

Until I moved to the Mission five years later, I could not remember the shop's name. The exterior had changed, but the interior stayed the same, reminding me of the personal memory.

The family-owned Mitchell's has been a San Francisco institution for more than sixty years. Located on the border of the Mission and Bernal Heights neighborhoods, the nearby block reflects an early San Francisco, with its classic Victorian-style buildings. History is pervasive here. At the turn of the century, the Mitchell family's matriarch owned the entire building—a brazen responsibility for women at the time. She leased the retail location to a liquor store. After World War II, the space became vacant. Inspired by Garrett's, a popular ice cream shop and local dairy farm, the young Mitchell brothers opened an ice cream shop. In those days, families in San Francisco owned their own farms—where they processed dairy and operated the pasteurization process. Ice cream was the logical next step.

The Mitchell family adapts to changing times. Italian and Polish populated the neighborhood. Then Asian and Mexican residents increased. Connected with a business that imports produce from the Philippines, the Mitchell family was inspired to create ice cream flavors that better matched their changing clientele. Customers are astounded how well the ice cream recreates their memories of buko (young coconut), ube (purple yam), and guava. Especially mango, the most popular flavor at Mitchell's.

Walking to the shop before its opening embodies the typical San Francisco morning. Late-waking workers of prominent Silicon Valley companies run to catch their last shuttle. Bikes tumble down the streets—the fixed-gears and classic cruisers with riders wearing messenger bags emblazoned with silver buckles. The parklet, a mini city-sanctioned park instituted to reduce car congestion, at San Jose Avenue and Guerrero Street is empty, but will fill up later with ice cream lovers.

In front of the shop, a lone white refrigerated truck pulls up, ready for the day's orders. Requests for the ice cream arrive from all over the city. Restaurants, cafes, grocery stores, and events want to partake in the ice cream.

Employees spill outside. One pulls up the curtains, revealing posters advertising the flavors and special concoctions. With that flourish, the shop is open. Bright white, glass display cases present flavors from the very basic vanilla and chocolate to the more exotic ones like ube and mango. On the windows and walls, posters highlight specials like halo halo, a Filipino dessert, and Baseball Nut Sundae, a tribute to the San Francisco Giants, the local baseball team.

Behind a door, an Emery-Thompson ice cream machine hums and churns fifteen batches per day, except on Sunday when half that amount is done. Premade custards pour into the machine. White plastic bins of fresh ube and coconut sit ready to flavor the batch. With precision, an ice cream maker quickly lifts a bin and pours it in at the last few minutes of churning. The white base transforms to purple and tastes tropical. Like clockwork, an employee places a half-gallon orange carton underneath a spout and pumps a handle, releasing the soft mixture. The employee thumps the carton to distribute the soft ice cream, pushes a cap on and adds it to a growing stack. He repeats the process over and over until the batch is complete. Another employee takes the stack and moves it into a nearby freezer, where it will remain until it is needed.

Famous for a high butterfat of 16% in their creamy ice cream, Mitchell's is known for its tropical flavors. Excelling at these tastes led to a common misconception that the Mitchell's owners are Filipino.

"I have a serious sweet tooth," Linda Mitchell begins. "Lots of people ask if I would be sick of ice cream. And I am not."

She peers at me over an old wooden desk. Linda and her brother Brian manage Mitchell's. Her father Larry is one of the brothers who founded Mitchell's and has let his children run the day-to-day operations. Linda's auburn chin-length hair shakes as she gestures. Her conversation reflects a complex experience of being the owner's child and a current manager of more than twenty years. She formerly worked in banking, but returned to the family business to join Brian, responsible for flavor development. "Everyone knows that I am going to be practical," she acknowledges her past professional life.

We are in the Mitchell's office, adjacent to the ice cream shop. The office, a former studio reminiscent of the tiny 200 square foot apartments of New York, has mostly bare walls and little furniture, a sharp contrast to the shop filled with posters declaring new exciting flavors and concoctions.

"Horchata!" she exclaims when I ask about her last ice cream scoop. "Because I felt like it."

I tell her about how I first found the place. She smiles. In the days before smartphones, my sister and I were not the only ones burdened with misdirection—many a lost driver arrived at Mitchell's. Even today, they arrive lost. The shop has also served as the choice for first dates, informal gatherings for friends and family, and innocent rewards after a long day at work.

"Every day felt amazing," Linda described her work at Mitchell's. "People are happy when they have ice cream."

Eucalyptus Ice Cream

Combine cornstarch and 2 ½ tablespoons of the cream in a small bowl. Mix, until there are no lumps, to create a cornstarch slurry.

Combine with the remaining cream, milk, sugar, and salt in a medium saucepan. Place over medium heat. When the mixture begins to steam, add the cornstarch slurry. Continue to stir until the mixture thickens.

Remove from heat and pour into a large bowl. Add the eucalyptus leave pieces to steep. Chill the mixture for at least 12 hours in the refrigerator to enhance the flavor.

Strain out the eucalyptus leave pieces. Churn in an ice cream maker following manufacturer's instructions.

Scoop eucalyptus ice cream into an empty resealable container. Freeze up to a month. To serve, let stand at room temperature until slightly softened, about 10 minutes. When serving, optionally drizzle honey over the ice cream.

2

Seattle

"You might say that I moved here for love," Adria, the owner of Parfait Ice Cream, said while she laughed.

The ice cream maker was not the only one to say that about Seattle. I have heard the same phrase from friends and strangers. This northwest city, nestled within viewing distance of the green Cascade Range, Mount Rainier, and Puget Sound, exudes a love of nature. Outsiders say it's "cold and wet," but that concept is a trade-off for the beautiful summers and easy access to water sports.

Influenced by the Slow Food movement in the San Francisco Bay Area and Seattle's proximity to fresh produce, the food culture emphasizes local, organic ingredients. Starting sometime in 2006, the neighborhood of Capitol Hill was transformed into a "capital of ice cream" and a "walk of dessert." Within a five-block area, an ice cream lover can now find gelato, frozen custard, and handmade small batches of ice cream.

Love of Seattle comes in the form of a romance with the easy-going locals, the brilliant sunsets across the sound, the vibrant indie music scene on Broadway Avenue, the obsession with coffee, and the affordability of the city. Families often move here for a big city environment, but with a lower cost of living. Within the headquarters of Microsoft and Amazon, Seattle residents give off a technological vibe as they carry their Kindles and smartphones (not just iPhones). Food trucks can be found all over the city. Foodies are abundant throughout the area, writing reviews on Yelp, Foursquare, and other social-based services.

An ice cream maker remembers the day when his school-age son visited his shop with friends. The son pointed to his father and said, "That's my dad. He makes ice cream."

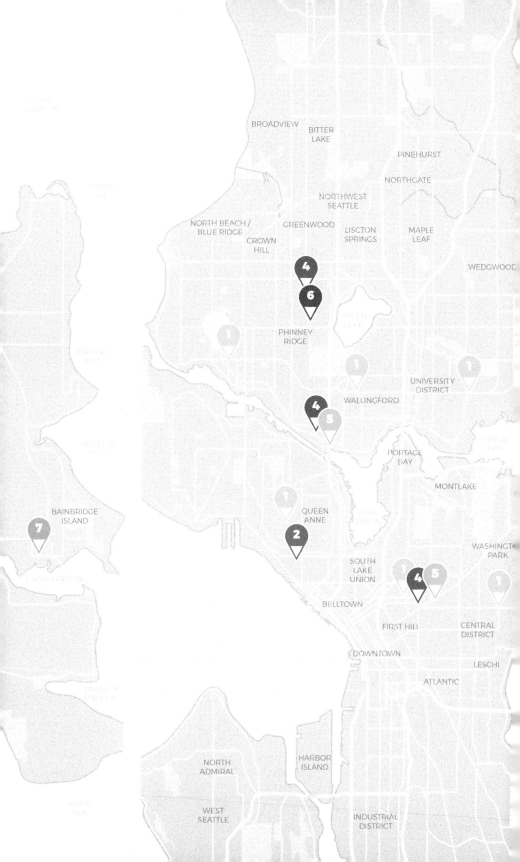

Molly Moon's Homemade Ice Cream

mollymoonicecream.com

1622 1/2 N 45th St
(206) 547-5105

917 E Pine St
(206) 708-7947

1408 34th Ave
(206) 324-0753

321 W Galer St
(206) 457-8854

2615 NE 46th St
(206) 525-5140

522 19th Ave E
(206) 735-7970

Social Ice Cream

enjoysocial.net

Roving location and hours

501 2nd Ave W

Parfait Ice Cream

parfait-icecream.com

2034 NW 56th St
(206) 258-3066

Bluebird Microcreamery

bluebirdseattle.com

1205 E Pike St
(206) 588-1079

7400 Greenwood Ave N
(206) 588-6419

3515 Fremont Ave N
(206) 588-1079

Old School Frozen Custard

oldschoolfrozencustard.com

1316 E Pike St
(206) 324-2586

704 N 34th St
(206) 695-2887

Half Pint Ice Cream

halfpinticecream.com

Roving location and hours

67 Phinney Ave N

Mora Iced Creamery

moraicecream.com

39 Madrone Ln N
Bainbridge Island, WA
(206) 855-1112

Parfait Ice Cream

Parfait is the only organic ice cream in Seattle, started by a pastry chef. Starting as a food truck serving small batch ice cream and uniquely housemade cones, Parfait has opened a brick and mortar store.

parfait-icecream.com

2034 NW 56th St

(206) 258-3066

"You can say that I moved here for love," Adria Shimada says and laughs.

She perches on a stool in Cookspace, a cooperative kitchen in the lower Queen Anne neighborhood. Adria wears a black dress that coordinates with her black beret; the beret is slightly tilted on her brunette hair. Cookspace is a large kitchen space that is located inside a one-floor warehouse. I had imagined that the kitchen would slowly fill up in a few hours with pastry chefs kneading dough, and assistants moving bins from freezer to refrigerator. I was wrong. Now, in the early summer morning at 6 AM, the warehouses and residences seem to be waiting until their occupants and workers wake up. Adria has been awake for several hours, taking care of her toddler son. Even so, her enthusiasm bubbles out easily as she recounts stories of cooking. "I want to maintain personal integrity," Adria says about how she makes ice cream using good ingredients.

Knowing my love of food trucks, my friends took me to the 2012 Mobile Food Truck Rodeo event in Seattle. Food trucks parked in a huge circle in the Fremont neighborhood. I sampled bites from a Southern Style BBQ truck to the Japanese Hot Dog truck. Feeling greasy from the fried food we had just eaten, we pounced onto the ice cream trucks.

Even after more than a year, Parfait sticks out in my memory, as if it had cut through the fat of fried mac-n-cheese and grilled hot dogs. The truck was painted with butterflies dancing around orange chrysanthemums on a chocolate brown background. Then the flavors: from Earl Grey tea to strawberry. The strawberry flavor had a delicate taste of just-picked fruit and milk, which was both floral and elegant. Ice cream is served on housemade cones, decorated with pressed intricate designs. I remember thinking, "*That* ice cream, I will remember."

Adria's path toward ice cream started with a year abroad in Europe. At the time, she was studying English literature at Cornell University and was uncertain about her future. In France, she tasted ice cream made at the famous Berthillon creamery. Then she moved to a farm stay near Toulouse, where she assisted a chef. She observed that French chefs valued quality ingredients, fruit picked at their height of flavor, and making foods from scratch. Adria observed that ice cream was served in cones, in small portions, allowing the customers to indulge but not over-indulge. This was unlike America where ice cream had become industrialized using syrups and processed ingredients.

In San Francisco, she studied to be a pastry chef at the California Culinary Academy. After graduation, she worked at the popular French bakery, La Farine, and the Bay Area vegetarian institution, Greens Restaurant. But she wanted to do something more creative than making baked goods.

It started when Adria followed her husband back to his hometown of Seattle. To her surprise, she noticed that many food shops in Seattle lacked the same culinary values as a high-end bakery like La Farine and ice cream shops like Ici Ice Cream, both institutions of the Slow Food movement. With her new-found awakening to natural, homemade food, Adria decided to start her own ice cream business, because it offered a blank canvas for experimentation.

Starting with a food truck, she began serving ice cream. Unlike having a shop, using a food truck means that everything must be pre-packed and stored at the right temperature. "With the truck, we can reach more people," Adria says. "It is crazy and exciting. The truck could break down, or it could have a flat tire. Anything can happen."

Raw ingredients are core to everything that Parfait makes. While many ice cream shops use a pre-made ice cream base (often created at a dairy plant and consisting of milk, cream, and sugar), Adria invests the energy to create her own ice cream base that is customized to each flavor. By maintaining ownership over the base, she produces a better flavor infusion rather than using a pre-made base where the cream and milk ratio is the same for all flavors. Adria steeps the milk and cream with lavender before mixing them together with sugar. The basic mint ice cream is made with fresh spearmint leaves that are steeped in milk for more than one day. All confections and mix-ins are made in-house including the cones and toffee. "It's hard work to do it from scratch," Adria says. "But I choose to do it."

Focusing on making the highest quality products does come with some sacrifices. Her ice cream is more expensive than others in the area. Also, the ice cream batches take longer to make because of the raw ingredients and the steeping of flavors. Having pure and perfect flavors means that she uses expensive raw fruit.

Adria remembers the early days of Ben & Jerry's, during the 70s and 80s. Back then she had tried the *Wanilla!* ice cream, a blend of vanilla and strawberry flavors. It was a flavor so intense that its taste is still lodged in her memories. Despite their goals of expansion, Adria observed that they continued to make their ice cream with the same values, thereby showing that big dreams do not require a sacrifice in integrity.

Adria concocts her own unique ice cream flavors; many are inspired by local ingredients. She likes honey rose ice cream, made with honey, organic roses, and infused rosewater. Fresh blueberries are folded into her ice cream. One flavor is cinnamon toast ice cream, and although a cereal shares the name, she prefers the intensity and homegrown flavor of her ice cream. Adria prizes the butter toffee crunch flavor, which embodies the *ethos* of her philosophy with housemade toffee and butter infusion. It is all made from scratch. "Ice cream is my healthy alternative food," she says. "But it's a small treat! Because ice cream can't be ice cream with some fat."

She smiles while she glances at a protégé who is working across the room at Cookspace, busily straining freshly roasted peaches. This is Adria's kitchen. This is where raw, whole ingredients combine to make the signature Parfait ice cream. Adria leans forward and says in a whisper, "When I was twenty, I had a favorite ice cream shop. I went back there recently, and I was disappointed. My ice cream tastes better."

Bluebird Microcreamery

Bluebird started when the founder discovered that ice cream shops were uncommon throughout Seattle as he wandered the streets in 2008. Pairing with a local brewery, the first shop opened in Capitol Hill, serving beer flavors and encouraging community.

bluebirdseattle.com

1205 E Pike St

(206) 588-1079

7400 Greenwood Ave N

(206) 588-6419

3515 Fremont Ave N

(206) 588-1079

Somehow, everywhere I went in Seattle, I came across a Bluebird Microcreamery. The first Bluebird Microcreamery was built along the "ice cream corridor" of the Capitol Hill neighborhood, where hipsters roamed the thrift shops and independent furniture design stores. Couches and board games huddle in a corner, inviting customers to hover over coffee, ice cream, or beer. Dark wood throughout the space suggests a dimly-lit pub-like atmosphere, although instead of drinking, the customers sink into couches, licking their ice cream.

In contrast to the Capitol Hill shop, the other Bluebird Microcreamery shops are small and brightly lit. In the Fremont neighborhood, the shop has space for a long counter and a few chairs, and it caters to office workers; in the Greenwood location, this location attracts local families. In that shop, I order a simple vanilla scoop in a dish. The scooper, who has a friendly face framed with curly hair pulled back in a ponytail, chats about her summer. Her name is Ashley. I am sitting on a small milk jug near a large window. My feet barely touch the hardwood floors made from reclaimed wood. The ice cream flavors are written in colored chalk on a blackboard. Children energized from their school day pull their parents into the doorway as they walk by the large windows. The Greenwood shop's environment and design are the embodiment of Josh Reynolds' vision of Bluebird Microcreamery.

A picture of a bluebird is painted in the store - it is the logo of Bluebird Microcreamery. Not far from the bluebird logo, I spot a picture of the Bluebird Microcreamery truck. The actual vintage white milk truck came from Iowa, where it was used to delivered Dairy Gold products to customers during the 1940s and 50s. The side of the truck is painted with a bluebird that is perched on the word "Bluebird."

Josh, the founder, rushes into the shop, coming from a music event where Bluebird Microcreamery was hired to make a custom ice cream flavor. He is busy, managing partnerships with bands like Phantagram and Girl Talk to promote Bluebird. Success is easy now.

Yet, ice cream was not always easy to find in Seattle. The process for Josh started in the summer of 2007. While strolling after dinner, Josh suggested to his friend, "Let's grab dessert."

His friend gave him an empty stare and said, "Dessert?"

Accustomed to locals hanging out at ice cream stands on the East Coast, Josh realized that Seattle lacked a place where locals could congregate informally around dessert. During his childhood summers in the Northeast, he would travel thirty-two miles to upstate New York to Camp Chingachgook on Lake George. On the way, ice cream shops dotted roadside landscapes. Whenever he could, he would get a cone. Josh loved the birthday cake ice cream flavor at Stewart's, found only in upstate New York and Vermont. Stewart's ice cream flavors were not gourmet, yet they encouraged the customers to hang out and build a community.

Today, Josh is wearing a Camp Chingachgook t-shirt, a hand-drawn green pine tree overlaying a bright red triangle. Sitting on a milk jug, Josh looks like he belongs in the wilderness, going on long hikes like he did during his childhood summers. Josh glances at Ashley, who has just cheerfully scooped ice cream for a small family. "That's where I met Josh," she says from across the room. "He convinced me to move to Seattle to help him with Bluebird."

After the summer of 2007, Josh started to work on his dream. Having made ice cream successfully for friends and family, he knew that he was on to a compelling idea. "I wasn't married, and I didn't have kids," Josh says. "It was the right time to do it."

Digging into his life savings, Josh began forming the business. To stay within his budget, he built nearly everything by hand. The furniture in his first shop came from thrift stores, donations, and scrap materials. Josh followed a do-it-yourself philosophy by gathering his own materials and by seeking help through his community. He convinced his friends to join him. "It's easy to make friends in Seattle," Josh says. "Everyone wants to help out."

He contacted ice cream shops for advice. The owner of the Blue Marble Creamery in New York City sent him a manifesto that had been passed through ice cream shops. One of the manifesto's premises is that in the United States, ice cream is considered a "to-go" item because customers prefer to lick their ice cream while they stroll; nobody sits to eat ice cream. "So, did shops really need seating?" Josh asks aloud. "I mean, will people stick around anyway?"

"What I learned the most from the manifesto is, if you want to have great ice cream, don't stray from the principles," Josh says. "I want people to say, 'Bluebird—this is a Seattle store'."

Using local, high-quality ingredients and having community support are the principles that guide the business. The ingredients come from places within a one-hour drive from Seattle, like the chocolate from Theo Chocolate and the coffee from cafes like Caffe Vita. Flavors reflect the season like pumpkin and ginger for the winter. Another popular ice cream flavor uses the award-winning stout from the neighboring Elysian Brewery. Words like "fair trade", "grass-fed", and "organic" sprinkle Josh's sentences. "I support my neighbors," Josh says. "I don't do cheap."

"Last week, I heard that someone in Minnesota tasted my ice cream," Josh says and smiles. "She said, 'That's Bluebird!'"

For his Greenwood store, Josh dreamed of having a research and development laboratory with a large window where adults and children could see the magical brewing process. In addition to the housemade brew, specialty sodas will be made, with flavors like cinnamon and birch sarsaparilla. Walking down a small stairway at the back of the Greenwood shop, we enter the microbrewery. A large reclaimed freezer is ready for work. Kegs stand prepared to brew beer. Construction is about to begin to build the window for his customers. "I am excited," Josh says.

Even with the success of Bluebird Microcreamery, Josh still continues to listen to the community's ideas. Ideas for ice cream flavors come from everyone—his customers, his staff, and the world. New recipes are created after diligent research. Then Josh looks for feedback. "Community" is a word that echoes through Josh's conversations.

Josh learned from his father, who was a doctor, to always praise his employees. Most importantly, Josh maintained his father's primary guiding principle. Josh says, "We should always help our friends."

Half Pint Ice Cream

Half Pint is the first ice cream in Seattle to sell at local Seattle farmers markets. The one-woman show features a rotating menu of flavors from locally sourced farmers.

halfpinticecream.com

Roving location and hours

67 Phinney Ave N

In a corner of the farmers market, the sign lists the organic ice cream flavors of the day: orange chocolate, Earl Grey chocolate, peach sorbet, and cinnamon cookie. On previous days the list was vanilla-chocolate, lemon vanilla, toasted coconut, and berry sorbet. Nearby stands burst with baskets of juicy blueberries, fresh strawberries, and fuzzy peaches—they punctuate the air with a rainbow-like aroma. Soon, the produce here will become ice cream flavors at Half Pint Ice Cream. One stand offers overripe berries that will not sell, and within a few days, the berries will used at Half Pint. Another vendor has picked too many peaches, and as the market day ends, the unsold peaches end up at Half Pint, becoming the next day's peach sorbet.

Cle Franklin, the sole owner of Half Pint Ice Cream, serves a family. First, she gives a scoop of chocolate ice cream to the bouncing child and then a scoop of peach sorbet to his mother. Cle's brunette hair is smartly pulled back, and she wears a colored t-shirt. As the mother and son take their cones, Cle talks to them for a long time about their day and their journey to the farmers market. This is not unusual. She knows all of the regular customers by name—they are the shoppers who grab fresh produce and then head for her stand. "This way I get only one self-indulgent treat every week," one of the regulars says. "It's my favorite day!"

Cle grew up in Boston. Her parents, who are business owners, encouraged her to develop an entrepreneurial spirit. The long driveway that led to her house served as a playground for her to grow her business ideas, like selling mint water and friendship bracelets. Later, she worked in food-related jobs at coffee shops. In the Boston area, her love of ice cream played a large part in her life, and she indulged in her favorite treat on a daily basis. Outside of Boston, in Jamaica Plain, she worked at J.P. Licks, the famous local ice cream chain, where she learned that an oval-shaped ice cream scoop made scooping easy. Most importantly, Cle learned how excellent customer service and great ice cream work together to make happy customers.

After she moved to Seattle, she noticed a dearth of homemade ice cream shops. She missed her traditional summer outings of going out for her favorite food. She asked herself, "Was Seattle's famous rain the reason for the lack of great ice cream shops?" Then a thought occurred to her, "Can I change that?"

With little experience in starting or running a food business, Cle rushed into her own venture. She opened Half Pint Ice Cream in 2006, the same year when other ice cream shops opened like Bluebird and Molly Moon's. With her own ice cream maker, Cle started making ice cream to fill Seattle's then empty dessert niche. Because she wasn't ready to open her own shop immediately, she started selling at the local farmers markets. "It's fun to to be outside," Cle says. "Who doesn't want that?"

She found a cooperative kitchen at Cookspace, which she used as her home base. Cookspace is unique because of its nature as a cooperative kitchen built for food entrepreneurs. Since she started using the Cookspace kitchen, Cle has been the longest running tenant, and she returns year after year. The cooperative spirit of the Cookspace kitchen encourages the owners of ice cream businesses to get along. The owners agreed, "Let's not have weirdness—let's help each other."

Half Pint Ice Cream is found at the weekday markets, which open in the late afternoon. Cle learned that Seattle residents used their mornings for running errands, and their afternoons for "hanging out"—and a better time for selling ice cream. She experimented with selling ice cream at morning weekend markets in the hope that a long, leisurely stroll would lead shoppers to pause for an ice cream break. But shoppers were not interested in ice cream in the morning. Cle chooses sell only at afternoon markets, because ice cream lovers could have ice cream twice in one day—a scoop at the market and a take-home container at home.

Studying the total sales throughout the year, Cle discovered that ice cream sells best when Seattle residents are relaxed in warm temperatures. Half Pint Ice Cream operates seasonally; it sells ice cream only six to seven months out of the year, depending on how soon winter starts in the temperate climate of Seattle. The four best ice cream months usually occur somewhere between April and October.

When she is not working, Cle spends her time-off to do more research about ice cream, traveling to Hawaii for some tropical inspiration, and visiting her family in the East Coast.

Half Pint Ice Cream is invited to cater private events. "I catered an ice cream party at a wedding!" Cle gushes. "It helped me break out of my routine. But having good customer service actually matters a lot," she says. "People remember that most of all."

"I worry that I will forget something," Cle says. "Will the ice cream melt today? Will a disaster happen? Will there be scrambled eggs in my ice cream? It's like life or death."

She frowns as she remembers the $1,500 refrigerator that was her first purchase. Excited, she plugged it in, not realizing that it required a special electric current. The refrigerator was destroyed. She smiles again and laughs about the time she accidentally mixed sanitization liquid with the ice cream blend. She straightens up and says emphatically, "It happens."

Mora Iced Creamery

Mora, based in Bainbridge Island, was started by an Argentine family inspired by their country's ice cream culture. Ice cream flavors like dulce de leche and mora (blackberry) evoke strong memories of their home country for South American visitors.

moraicecream.com

39 Madrone Ln N

Bainbridge Island, WA

(206) 855-1112

"I am going to have some Mora today," Jerry Perez says. "That's what I want people to think." Ana Orselli, his wife, smiles. "It's Mora, not just ice cream."

The Mora Iced Creamery husband and wife team dresses casually, blending in with the customers—parents, grandparents, couples, and schoolchildren. Parents with strollers rush into the shop.

"But you know, here at Mora, people can lower their guards," Ana says. "Adults behave like kids."

"Maybe they don't notice," Jerry says and laughs. "But we do."

Taking the advice of local Seattle friends, I rent a bike at the Bainbridge Island ferry dock and ride through the winding roads. Art fills the front yards with colorful stained glass sculptures and clanging wind chimes. Houses crowd the coast for waterfront views of downtown Seattle. Along a highway, a blueberry farm beckons a passerby. The slow life on the island is bucolic, a world away from the busy Seattle life across the water. Retirees squabble at the golf course, and children stream out of the school buses. Cars politely line up for the entrance to the ferry. When I return to the bike shop, the owner is not in. He has taped a note to the door of his office: "Leave the bike out front. Nobody will take it."

This island is home for many. Looking to move to Seattle from Argentina, it was this very island that captured the hearts of Jerry and Ana. As a child in Argentina, Jerry followed the Seattle Supersonics, his favorite basketball team. Although the team moved out of Seattle by the time he was ready to relocate, Jerry kept the dream of Seattle in mind. Stumbling upon Bainbridge Island one Halloween, he and Ana found their home. Because they both loved and missed the close-knit communities they had in Buenos Aires, they wanted to create an experience where people could build a community. "We figured that we wanted to live the American dream," Jerry says. "America is a nation of people creating extraordinary things."

Ice cream, much like the famous Argentine ice cream, was the right fit. This was the beginning of Mora Iced Creamery.

Sitting on one of the wooden benches outside of Mora Iced Creamery, Ana and Jerry fawn over the stream of customers. As parents of two daughters, they value family. On my visit, the first day of school has just ended. Parents reward their children with ice cream for the first day of school. The children smile gleefully as their scoop of Mora arrives.

The shape of the blackberry ("mora" means blackberry in Spanish) echoes inside the shop. Bunches of small dots resembling a blackberry pepper the walls and the paper ice cream cups. Young scoopers in black Mora caps stroll along the counter, offering customers smiles and

tastes of the sweet delights. "Have as many samples as you would like," they say.

"I am so lucky to have such great people working at Mora," Ana says. "Everyone is just so amazing."

Starting with a small shop on a main street, they started to sell ice cream to the community. As the business grew, they remodeled the store, while strengthening the Mora brand. Now, with two additional stores in nearby cities of Kingston and Poulsbo, their thoughts turn to franchising. They plan with due diligence, finding the right business partners as carefully as they would find a marriage partner.

Working with a food scientist, each ice cream flavor is tested repetitively until it reaches perfection. The shop began with forty-eight flavors; now, the number of flavors has grown to more than eighty. Flavors include smooth Swiss chocolate, locally sourced pistachio, mojito, Americana apple pie, and exotic green tea. The Earl Grey flavor a subtle bergamot aroma as it floats upward to the roof of my mouth. The fresh apricot flavor envelops my tongue. Although the most popular flavor is Mora's namesake, blackberry, Ana and Jerry think it's not fair to pinpoint a single flavor. Every flavor is crafted for someone to love it.

Each flavor is stored in a *pozzetta*, a small, temperature-controlled metal canister designed to protect the quality of the ice cream. "Customers don't realize that they have never seen the *pozzettas*," Ana says. "If they can sample as much as they want, then we're not taking anything away from their experience."

"We want people to eat using all of their senses!" Jerry adds.

"Someone asked me if we made bubble gum ice cream," Ana says. "But we just don't make that kind of flavor."

The word "artificial" does not exist at Mora. Coming from Argentina,

Jerry and Ana were surprised by the way Americans made cake batter from Betty Crocker mixes and that using food coloring was the norm. "We squeeze every lemon by hand," Jerry says. "There's a big different in quality when you use real fruit."

Jerry and Ana tell their favorite stories, one following another. They remember the visitor from Montana who cried when she tasted the *dulce de leche*, because the flavor reminded her of her home country of Argentina, a land she had not visited for years.

Ana tells her own story of two people who were in love—a Romeo-and-Juliet-like story. Coming from different European countries, political and religious laws kept them apart. Fearing retribution from their families, they chose Mora Iced Creamery as a safe place to meet. Once they were free, and away from judgment and danger, they shared a scoop together, on Bainbridge Island.

Then, Jerry launches into a story of a woman who was dying of cancer. She had a small request—to have some *dulce de leche* ice cream from Mora Iced Creamery. Her brother got the scoop of ice cream and brought it to her. She took a small spoonful, bringing it slowly to her lips. Upon tasting the ice cream, she smiled. Her brother took a snapshot and sent it to Ana and Jerry, thanking them for bringing a small moment of happiness through the darkness. Jerry still has the picture of the smiling woman, reminding him of the reasons why he started Mora Iced Creamery.

"Mora brings people together," Ana says. "[Having] Mora is just a simple, sweet happy thing to many people."

"We are so blessed and thankful for the community," Jerry adds and gazes at the line of customers.

Roasted Strawberry and Carmelized Banana Ice Cream

Preheat the oven to 375 degrees. Mix strawberries and ¼ cup sugar in a baking dish. Roast for 8 minutes or until soft. Cool. Puree with the lemon juice. Set aside.

Combine bananas and brown sugar in a medium pan. Mix together with a fork until fully mashed. Cook under medium heat for about 6 minutes until light brown. Cool. Puree to get an uniform texture. Set aside.

Combine cornstarch and 2 ½ tablespoons of the cream in a small bowl. Mix, until there are no lumps, to create a cornstarch slurry.

Whisk the remaining sugar, remaining cream, milk, and salt in a medium saucepan set over medium heat. When the mixture begins to steam, add the cornstarch slurry. Continue to stir until the mixture thickens, about 1 minute.

Chill the mixture at least three hours or overnight in a refrigerator.

Once the mixture is fully chilled, mix the strawberry puree and banana puree into the ice cream base. Scrape cold mixture into a pre-frozen ice-cream-maker bowl and churn according to manufacturer's instructions.

Scoop ice cream into an empty resealable container. Freeze up to a month. To serve, let stand at room temperature until slightly softened, about 10 minutes. Serve as is, or with fruit toppings like banana slices and strawberry slices.

3

Los Angeles

Growing up in Northern California, Los Angeles was the closest land of magic, just over 400 miles south of my childhood home. Some come for the dream of acting. Some come for the better weather. Some come for a cleaner lifestyle. Some come for better opportunities. With a touch of the camera lens and storytelling, anybody could be anything. Los Angeles may be known as La La Land, but when the dream is food, it is real.

With diverse immigrant groups, this world of glamour and beaches also filled with gourmet food. My Asian food-loving roots led me to steaming noodle bowls during the summer in the eastern Los Angeles suburbs and a burgeoning food truck scene near Venice Beach. Pinkberry, the shop that started the tart frozen yogurt craze? In Los Angeles first. An ice cream sandwich truck founded by a former architect student? In Los Angeles, of course! Where can you find true Persian ice cream? Yes, flavors of saffron and rose are ready at hand! A young man who opened a branch of Scoops, an ice cream shop known for a reclusive chef? Yes, the student did it by bonding with the chef over their common Korean roots. The invention of ice cream mochi, a twist on the traditional sweet Japanese rice cake? Frances Hashimoto, the late CEO of Mikawaya, and her husband Joel Friedman conceived of the treat in Japantown in Los Angeles, not in Hawaii or Japan as many believe. The year-round warm climate inspired a diverse set of ice cream treats and amazed the locals.

For many locals, Los Angeles doesn't just refer to the city of Los Angeles. It refers to the urban sprawl that extends from Pasadena to downtown Los Angeles to Santa Monica to Venice. Granted, many locals are concerned with the word "diet" (to me, I see "die" with a "t") and abhor the idea of a fatty calorie-filled indulgence. But when they indulge, oh they do indulge!

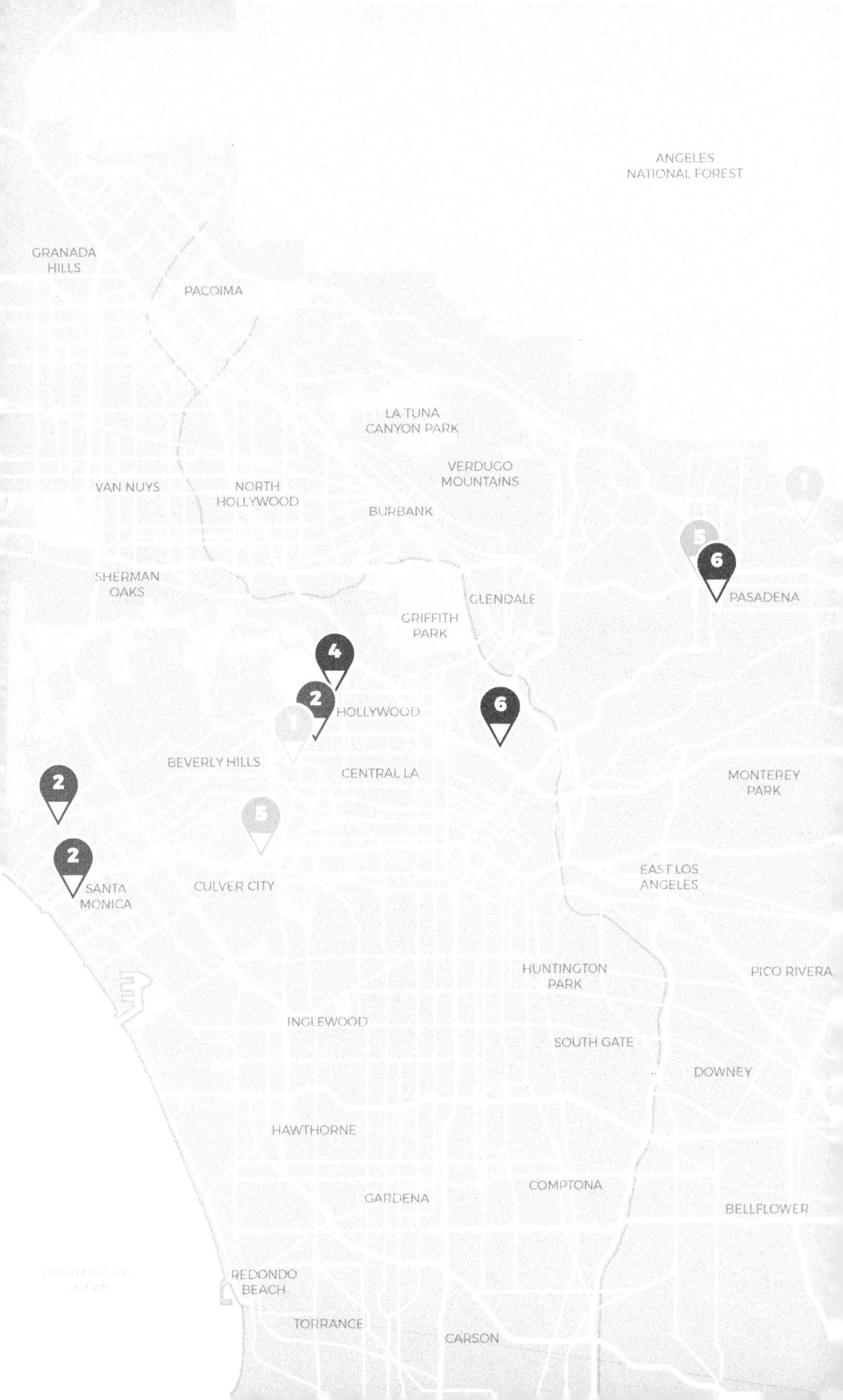
ANGELES
NATIONAL FOREST
GRANADA
HILLS
PACOIMA
LA TUNA
CANYON PARK
VERDUGO
MOUNTAINS
VAN NUYS
NORTH
HOLLYWOOD
BURBANK
SHERMAN
OAKS
GLENDALE
PASADENA
GRIFFITH
PARK
HOLLYWOOD
BEVERLY HILLS
CENTRAL LA
MONTEREY
PARK
SANTA
MONICA
CULVER CITY
EAST LOS
ANGELES
HUNTINGTON
PARK
PICO RIVERA
INGLEWOOD
SOUTH GATE
DOWNEY
HAWTHORNE
GARDENA
COMPTONA
BELLFLOWER
REDONDO
BEACH
TORRANCE
CARSON

Carmela Ice Cream

carmelaicecream.com

7920 W 3rd St
   Los Angeles, CA 90048
   (323) 944-0232

Sweet Rose Creamery

sweetrosecreamery.com

225 26th St #51
   Santa Monica, CA 90402
   (310) 260-2663
826 Pico Blvd
   Santa Monica, CA 90405
   (310) 260-2663
7565 Beverly Blvd
   Los Angeles, CA 90036
   (310) 260-2663

Neveux Artisan Creamery & Espresso Bar

neveuxartisancreamery.com

7407 Melrose Ave
   Los Angeles, CA 90046
   (323) 951-1002

Mashti Malone's Ice Cream

www.mashtimalone.com

1525 N La Brea Ave
   Los Angeles, CA 90046
   (323) 874-6168

Coolhaus

eatcoolhaus.com

Food truck roving location and hours
8588 Washington Blvd
   Culver City, CA 90232
   (310) 838-5559
59 E Colorado Blvd
   Pasadena, CA 91103
   (626) 486-2700

KindKreme

kindkreme.com

1700 Sunset Blvd
   Los Angeles, CA 90026
   (213) 989-1718
319 S Arroyo Pkwy
   Pasadena, CA 91105
   (877) 985-5463

Mashti Malone's

Mashti Malone's Ice Cream, located off of Sunset Boulevard in Hollywood, is a Persian ice cream shop serving exotic flavors like saffron and rosewater. Started by a stranded Iranian in the 1970s, he grew the business to serve the local Persian community and tickle the exotic tastes of foodies.

www.mashtimalone.com

1525 N La Brea Ave

Los Angeles, CA 90046

(323) 874-6168

"This reminds me of home," an Iranian-born college friend whispered in his softly accented English.

He had joined me on an excursion to Mashti Malone's Ice Cream, shortened to Mashti Malone's, in 2005. Back then, I had begun caring about the origins of food, and when Mashti Malone's popped up as a go-to destination in Los Angeles, I had to visit. We tasted saffron ice cream and ordered scoops of ice cream flavored with rosewater. No artificial ingredients existed here. My friend was instantly transported to his homeland where lavender, saffron, and rosewater reigned. A golden scoop of the eggless ice cream smelled of saffron—a taste of his culture and community. His eyes filled with tears, and he remembered his childhood city of Tehran, the capital city of Iran.

When I returned several years later, I become enraptured with that memory. I meet with Mehdi Shirvani, the current owner of Mashti Malone's, also originally from Iran. "I tell people to call me Matt," he says. "It's easier."

Tucked in a small strip mall off of Sunset Boulevard in Hollywood, Mashti Malone's escapes the consciousness of tourists and even locals. Quietly, it waits for a visit. One might notice the shop's presence with a towering sign next to large ice cream cone leaning on an equally sized four-leaf clover. Indeed, before exotic flavors became hip and a symbol of foodie status, the shop remained unnoticed. Delicate Persian script dances above "Mashti Malone's Ice Cream." When highlighted by Los Angeles food writers and featured on a segment on the Food Network in the early 2000s, tourists and tour buses descended. Hilary E. MacGregor's write-up in the Los Angeles Times in 2002 described, "an Iranian ice cream parlor, with flavors so exotic they sound like poetry, and ingredients that sound as if they must have been harvested from a Persian garden." This profile is credited for a rise in the popularity of Mashti Malone's.

During the day in February 2013, the shop is calm. For a moment. The walls capture a snapshot of liveliness. One wall presents playful red script framed in gold. Another details the ice cream specialties— mashti, faludeh, clone cone, and malone macaroon. A freezer hums in the background. Workers carry ingredients packaged in boxes, which make satisfying thumps as they are stacked. As the front doors open, the low traffic roar from Sunset Boulevard increases and fades as the doors shut. A taste of rose ice cream slides past my tongue, a floral scent deepening in my nostrils, and then fading. A young man in red basketball shoes moves items throughout the shop. An older man with graying hair laughs in Farsi and says one line in English, "Let me keep you busy."

Like many young Iranians in the seventies, Medhi's older brother Mashti moved to the United States for school. With the fall of the Shah in 1979, all connections to family in Iran were instantly severed. The

Iranian Revolution isolated citizens outside the country. Without steady financial support, Medhi's brother brainstormed alternatives. Back in Iran he had worked in the family food business, including servicing ice cream. So he worked as a chef and musician. Desiring connections with the stranded Persian community, he stumbled upon a closed ice cream shop started by Irish immigrants. In 1979, he purchased the shop with its original equipment. Lacking budget to update the sign, he compromised and changed half of the sign. With one half Irish and one half Persian, the shop became known as Mashti Malone's. Mehdi joined his brother in 1988 and helped grow the business using the same ice cream freezer and machine to this day.

Mashti Malone's struggled initially. Their location was not close to the Persian community, which were located in Beverly Hills and the San Fernando Valley. Eighty percent of their visitors are non-Persian— usually 20-45 year old young professionals. Visitors assumed that the ice cream came from India. Mehdi smiles as he tells his story—life in his homeland, the shop, the customer's initial fears of Persians, and the ice cream. He wears a blue polo shirt and leans back in his chair. Matt chuckles as he describes visitors' hesitations with the flavors. "Taste is changing," Mehdi says. "People are more adventurous. They used to just like mashed potatoes and gravy. People are hesitant to try."

He returns his thoughts to the present day. "Things have changed a lot! There's so much diversity in L.A. now." Mehdi gestures toward the list of flavors on the wall and says, "Everyone wants to try rosewater and faludeh."

Mehdi laments how Persian ice cream, even in Iran, has become westernized. Vanilla is the norm abroad. Yet, he credits American food marketing for the increased curiosity of his ice cream flavors. "POM Wonderful made it happen," he suggests, referring to the brand that popularized pomegranate juice. "Now people are willing to try the pomegranate sorbet."

Inspired, he has tried flavors like sour cherry and orange blossom. "I will see if people care for it," he says. "But I have limited space."

In his childhood in Iran, like all other kids, he loved sweets. Yet, little options for sweets existed. "It was very seasonal," he chuckles. "I would pay pennies to get a scoop. Now I can just get ice cream."

A filming crew nearby loved the shop so much that they gave a gift of signs, one with price and flavor list. Since then, the shop has catered many TV shows like *Everybody Loves Raymond* and *Happy Family*. "Even Mel Gibson knows us!" Mehdi says.

The Starline Tours bus, popular with Los Angeles visitors makes a special stop at the shop. Hollywood food tours visit Mashti Malone's, confirming its status as a continued destination for foodies.

The wholesale business suffered during the recession. Nearly 75% of the customers disappeared by the end of the recession. Despite the setback, Mehdi works to rebuild the wholesale business. He partnered with Whole Foods in California, Nevada, and Utah. "Now I cannot make enough ice cream!" he boasts. The planning and packing became a complicated process. Reluctantly, he moved production to an offsite facility in the nearby city of El Monte.

"Most people come happy," Mehdi says. "But all of them will leave happy. This is the cheapest anti-depressant pill."

Coolhaus

Coolhaus serves ice cream sandwiches. Inspired by great architecture, the founders aimed to create a treat that reflected their values in quality and community.

eatcoolhaus.com

Food truck roving location and hours

8588 Washington Blvd,

Culver City, CA 90232

(310) 838-5559

59 E Colorado Blvd.

Pasadena, CA 91103

(626) 486-2700

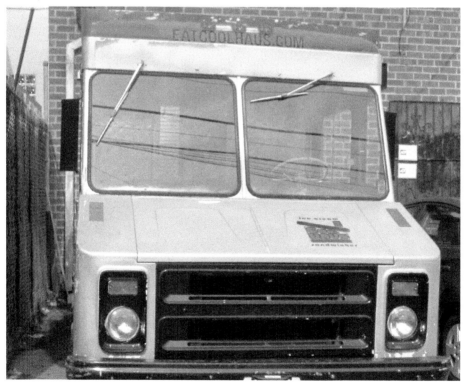

Once my friends and I move past the snarl of L.A. traffic to Culver City, we find Coolhaus, located across the street from the Studio Pali Fekete building. At the time of my visit in 2013, this is the sole brick and mortar location for the company, and the airy interior invites pedestrians from the concrete landscape. In the late morning, the sidewalks are empty. Road bikes with blue frames and pink rims are locked to meters. Tall palm trees break the concrete monotony. White exposed bricks frame the storefront of Coolhaus, and a blue logo in neon hangs in the corner. A large sticker—"Proudly Serving Blue Bottle Coffee Co"—clings to the main window. Inside, silver Mylar balloons spell out "Coolhaus." Indie rock music floats out of the loudspeakers, providing a beat that gently reverberates in the space. Near the door, a vertical freezer displays stacks of wrapped ice cream sandwiches. When the door opens, a male cashier pops up his head. A customer chooses a cookie flavor and an ice cream flavor. The cashier expertly puts the ice cream between two cookies and presents the result. The customer's face breaks into a childlike smile—unreserved delight that lights up the entire room.

This began in early 2009. When the recession hit, Natasha Case's short time at Disney Imagineering ended. After experiencing the wonder at Disney, she wanted to find something as meaningful. As a student of architecture for seven years, Natasha was heavily influenced by the philosophy of Rem Koolhaas, a well-known architect, and the

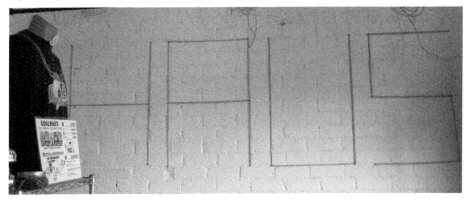

Bauhaus, a former well-respected German design school. In school, a professor observed the similarity between Natasha's models and layer cakes. Ice cream sandwiches, a frozen dessert that relies on cookies to give form, was her answer.

Quality food and architecture? Food + Architecture, or "Farchitecture"? Cool houses. Playing with the words, the name Coolhaus was born as a tribute to Koolhaas. Partnering with her girlfriend, Freya Estreller—an expert in real estate and operations—they created ice cream sandwiches. They combined originality with ecofriendliness and quality from local and organic ingredients. With persistence, they talked their way to launching at Coachella, an annual music festival in the California desert in Indio. Customers standing all day in the hot sun listening to pounding beats from their favorite bands? Perfect opportunity for ice cream!

From their 2014 cookbook, *The Coolhaus Cookbook*, they describe Coolhaus as "a thinker about reclaiming public and urban space for eating and gathering, when and where it is least expected" and "an architecture-inspired ice cream sandwich." Natasha and Freya brainstormed flavors, playing on their architectural influence with names like Frank Behry, a berry flavor, and Mintimalism, ice cream infused with whole mint leaves. "Like Ben & Jerry's Cherry Garcia, we wanted to look cool," Natasha remembers, and her floppy brown hat bobs as she describes the story.

Taking a risk, they financed everything on credit cards. The truck did not quite work and had to be towed to the festival. Despite all the challenges, the launch was a success. Popularity of food trucks was increasing then, and as the first food trucks present at the festival, they attracted thousands of young people, like themselves, to innocent refreshment. Everyone—over 100,000 people—clamored for the ice cream sandwiches. It was a wildfire. After the festival, *Curbed*, a Los

Angeles blog, wrote a post that included a link to their Twitter feed. New fans rushed to find the truck.

"People react to fire," Natasha says. "They just get drawn in. It was a news story."

The buzz was immediate, and the news of a burgeoning ice cream business burst onto the Los Angeles scene. *Dwell* and *Los Angeles Magazine* covered Coolhaus. Festivals asked for them. The number of followers on Twitter grew, spreading beyond Los Angeles. In 2014, Natasha was named to "Forbes' 30 Under 30" and "Zagat 30 Under 30" for her innovation in entrepreneurship.

Today, Coolhaus has expanded to Austin and New York City. Their products are now carried in local stores like Whole Foods. Opaque wrappers maintain the consistency in the sandwiches at their trucks, grocery stores, and their flagship store. By using the same recipes for their retail product, quality is never compromised.

Natasha smiles as she remembers her best memory: the day they launched in New York City on May 1, 2011. Lines stretched around the corner. Freya and Natasha were impressed by their fans' dedication. "At the end of the day, people go to the best spot," Natasha says.

To her, Los Angeles is a destination city. I am no exception. In June 2010, I planned for a Friday evening in Los Angeles, writing emails to local friends: "Probably will be in Venice somewhere between 9:45 pmish to 10:30 pmish. I'll call or text you otherwise! I am looking to try Coolhaus!"

With the social media savvy of my generation, I hopped onto Facebook to find out and came across "First Fridays" in Venice. Food trucks! And Coolhaus! I zipped to Abbot-Kinney Boulevard where trucks illegally parked and drew crowds of twenty-somethings. They filled the sidewalks, walking past closed boutique stores and sitting on

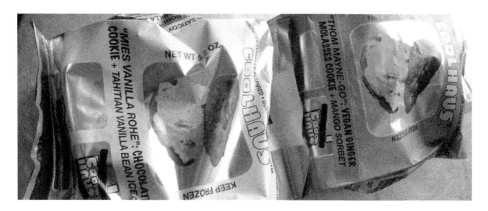

the ground. I jumped into the longest line at the festival. That summer night, lines snaked around a Korean taco truck, right past the BBQ food truck, and the mini sushi truck. The longest line was for Coolhaus, where I, of course, ordered an ice cream sandwich. The snickerdoodle cookie and mint ice cream tickled my tongue. With each bite, the cookie melded with the ice cream. This was the ideal ice cream truck.

Natasha rushes to a meeting with Freya, dressed in a black jacket over a blue button down. The shop is now calm. An iPhone plays music through the speakers overhead echoing the same musical acts that wafted to the Coolhaus truck at Coachella in 2009. Metal chairs and gray stools are scattered throughout the shop. Bright yellow utility lights stand in a corner. Natasha calls this the "showroom"—where Coolhaus shows its best self. It is the headquarters too, the place Freya and Natasha meet to work on the business. A Coolhaus truck sits a few blocks away, ready to load up ice cream sandwiches.

Natasha says, "Our product speaks well to everything."

KindKreme

KindKreme believes that everyone can have ice cream with flavors that are gluten-free, dairy-free, nut-free, and vegan. With locations throughout Los Angeles, their icekreme is served with savory cafe items.

kindkreme.com

1700 Sunset Blvd

Los Angeles, CA 90026

(213) 989-1718

319 S Arroyo Pkwy

Pasadena, CA 91105

(877) 985-5463

The raw vegan ice cream shop KindKreme caught my eye when I stopped by its branch in Pasadena. KindKreme believes that everyone can have ice cream with flavors that are gluten-free, dairy-free, nut-free, and vegan. The ingredients are all organic and locally sourced.

The flavors range from honey strawberry to chocolate nib. They are all raw, so the texture and consistency is different than normal ice cream, which is often cooked. Each scoop is sticky and slides down my throat with the smooth texture that I expect, but transforms into a deeper flavor. I do taste the absence of dairy. At the same time, the underlying fruits, nuts, and other ingredients burst to the surface. Strawberries fill my mouth, so it's like eating the whole fruit. The bite finishes off with the familiar sweet taste of honey. Intrigued, I email the owners immediately. Within the hour, Mollie calls and invites me to chat with her and her co-founder.

The ceiling of the Echo Park location is high, and the brick, exposed. Chocolate-colored windmills slowly spin overhead. A display case showcases the twelve flavors, a contrast to the over seventy flavors in the Pasadena location. Baskets of fruit lay on the counters. A nearby refrigerator stores the drinks. Indie music plays in the background. Songs by Feist and Passion Pit trickle through the airy space.

The customers are diverse. I spot a young twenty-something with a beard, a knotted ponytail, and tight jeans. An older family enjoys an early dinner in a corner. Voices mingle in and out again. Newly arrived diners study a tall menu trimmed in green. They relax in a typical Southern California style, taking their time to enjoy the fresh food and rest on the white chairs that emulate milk cans. The wood is dark and rustic with evidence of reclamation. Sunlight pours in through the tall windows, framed by bowed, long green curtains. Servers move through the space with flowing steps.

A young child with curly hair bounces in, making a beeline

directly for the display case showcasing ice cream, known as icekreme to emphasize its vegan quality. Her eyes scream *I want this. Now!* She presses her face against the glass and ogles the flavors. Following behind, two women appear in the doorway, carrying an attitude of knowing the space. They approach and introduce themselves as the owners of KindKreme.

Mollie Englehart, and her co-founder Mimi Moss finish each other sentences like best friends. They are natural complements and were housemates for three years. Before KindKreme was founded, Mollie experimented with raw ice cream. These recipes eventually became the staples in all the stores. Living in the same house, Mimi would sneak into the kitchen to have secret late night snacks from the icekreme. At the time, she pursued her dream of acting.

As a child of the founders of Cafe Gratitude, a popular Northern California raw vegan restaurant, Mollie is no stranger to the culture

and its strict dietary beliefs. What about the childhood delight of desserts? Traditional items like cupcakes are forbidden because they include eggs, shortening, and milk.

Mollie admits that she loves sweets, even as a child. "My dad would bring me to Ben & Jerry's downtown secretly just for an ice cream cone," she says. "My mom got so upset when she found out, because it isn't vegan. But I loved the ice cream."

"What was your favorite Ben & Jerry's flavor?"

"Cherry Garcia," Mollie pauses and chuckles. "Maybe Heath Bar Crunch." She goes on, "When we were coming up with this idea, I thought long and hard about the children . . .What if parents could bring their kids somewhere and not worry about whether the food had dairy, sugar, or gluten? That they could see sixteen flavors, toppings, sundaes, and not worry about it? That's what I wanted to create."

"Let's do ice cream," Mimi remembers. "I am a big foodie."

Mollie watches Mimi's daughter hungrily eating icekreme. "We never have lemon sorbet," she adds. "Lemon sorbet isn't my favorite. That should never be the only option."

Because of dyslexia, Mollie prefers working in the kitchen while Mimi focuses on the management side of the business. After making their decision, the pair opened a number of shops. Starting in Studio City, they expanded to Pasadena and Echo Park. Mimi was surprised by the cost of ingredients. She discovered that high traffic was needed to support a shop that sold dessert, so they paired KindKreme with a vegan restaurant for better profit.

For Mollie, her love and expertise is in creating the icekreme. She experiments with flavors incorporating seaweed, strawberries, dates, acai, goji berry, and coconut. Sometimes the pair worries about whether something should be classified as vegan—honey is a common debate.

They vary their offerings based on the season with squash making an annual appearance. They want to make a good dessert that emulates the tastes many cannot have. "Most of them work out good," Mollie says in her husky drawl.

"I want more icekreme!" the young child with curly hair interrupts when she finishes her bowl.

They are no strangers to common food allergies. Mimi calms her daughter and explains, "My daughter is allergic to dairy. We started the shop before she was born, and it is just so amazing that she doesn't have to skip out on this special childhood moment."

"Kids should never have to miss out," Mollie echoes.

On Mother's Day in 2010, a young boy named Jamie visited the shop. Because he is autistic, his diet did not include refined dairy or nuts. With KindKreme, he could enjoy the small moments of sweet desserts. "We remember that it's bigger moments in children's lives," Mollie says.

"What is your biggest surprise in the business?" I wonder.

"We are surprised how many people cannot have traditional ice cream due to lactose intolerance and diet restrictions due to health concerns," Mollie replies. They look at each other. Mimi adds, "People have said, 'You have changed my life.' Making this has really achieved happiness."

Kiwi Lime Sorbet

10 small to medium ripe kiwis

2 washed unwaxed whole small to
    medium limes

1 cup powdered sugar (if using
    granulated sugar, grind to
    about 10 seconds in a blender
    or for serving)

Cut up one lime into small ½ inch pieces including the peel. Remove all seeds. Add lime pieces to a blender. Add only the juice of the second lime. Add sugar. Blend until a thick puree forms. Small bits of the lime skin (like fresh zest) will be visible

Halve the kiwis. Scoop the kiwis with a spoon into the blender. If the kiwis are ripe, then it should be easy to scoop. If they are less ripe, consider adding additional sugar to offset the sour taste.

Puree the mixture again. Add more sugar to taste.

For best results, chill the mixture for a few hours, although the mixture can be churned immediately if at room temperature or cooler. Scrape mixture into a pre-frozen ice-cream-maker bowl and churn according to manufacturer's instructions.

The sorbet is best served immediately. To store, scoop kiwi lime sorbet into an empty resealable container. Freeze up to a month. To serve, let stand at room temperature until slightly softened, about 10 minutes.

4

Columbus and Around

"I would ask [my parents] for a dollar for a scoop of ice cream," my Ohio friend said. "Because then I could use the change to get candy!"

My friend's eyes became misty as she reminisced about her childhood. The residents of Columbus live a typical Midwestern American life. It's a place where pride for the local university reverberates. "I am a Buckeye fan," my friend said.

This statement represents the fervor of Columbus residents. Spirited friends, who grew up from Ohio, lament about the "state up north" and wax on about their love for Ohio State University—despite having not attended. The university symbolizes Columbus citizenship. Columbus may be dismissed "one of those college towns." With red banners and literal echoes of "Go Buckeyes!" throughout the town, outsiders see this place as football-obsessed. Ohio is where locals and new residents cling to their state-grown passions.

Ohio residents are obsessed about their local food favorites as much as they are obsessed about sports. With rich and fertile soil, agriculture and dairy farms dominate gentle, rolling hills. Homemade meals dominate the food scene. Food artisans are stubborn and insist on traditional methods. Resisting the ice cream industry's move to an automatic ice cream freezer, the Cincinnati-based Graeter's maintains a French pot process despite the additional time required to manually swirl each batch with a paddle. Johnson's Real Ice Cream stays small, catering to their neighborhood of Bexley, outside of Columbus.

But Jeni's Splendid Ice Creams is a main highlight. Jeni Britton Bauer, the owner of Jeni's, had dropped out of school to become an ice cream entrepreneur, crafting ice cream flavors with French cooking techniques. I admit that I failed to meet Jeni despite repeated phone calls, descriptive emails, a thorough reading of her detailed cookbook, and repeated visits to her Columbus-based shops. I tasted a sorbet made of wheatgrass and an ice cream swirled with roasted cherries and goat

cheese. I stalked her kitchen watching young, hair-netted employees handwrite flavors with sharpies on hundreds of tubs to be shipped across the country. A large metal freezer holds stacks of tubs, and Jeni's branded trucks with cheerful orange logos wait outside in the parking lot. Even a Jeni's brand ambassador, based in Washington D.C., never met her. My sister chased Jeni down in New York when Jeni was visiting for a food truck tour. They chatted about the artisanal nature of the vanilla bean, the shop's inspiring message, and the essence of her ice cream.

During my last few days in Ohio, in her kitchen and her shops, I discover that her philosophy embodies more than capturing flavors. Instead it extends to a quality ice cream experience. I sit on locally-designed furniture and taste flavors made with fresh ingredients, balancing sweetness and creaminess. Most importantly, Jeni's is about the relationship between the ice cream and the community. In November 2002, the biggest game of the year between the rivals Ohio State University and University of Michigan was happening at the university campus. Yet in North Market, the public market of Columbus, an unexpected crowd of fans formed for the opening day of the first Jeni's shop.

The following stories are about ice cream shops that celebrate this rich Ohio pride and the quality that we seek in our homemade food.

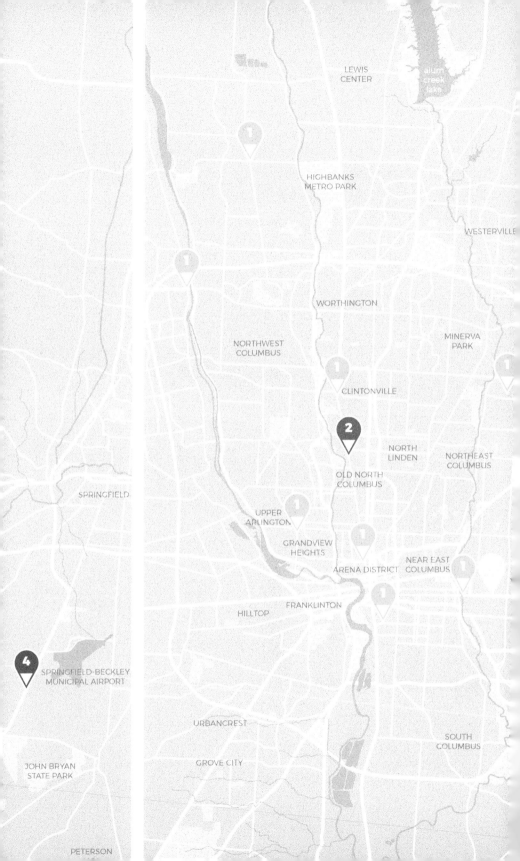

Jeni's Splendid Ice Creams

jenis.com

8 N Liberty St
Powell, OH 43065
(614) 846-1060

1 W Bridge St
Dublin, OH 43017
(614) 792-5364

4247 N High St
Columbus, OH 43214
(614) 447-0500

3998 Gramercy St
Columbus, OH 43219
(614) 476-5364

1281 Grandview Ave
Grandview Heights, OH 43212
(614) 488-2680

59 Spruce St
Columbus, OH 43215
(614) 228-9960

900 Mohawk St
Columbus, OH 43206
(614) 445-6513

2156 E Main St
Bexley, OH 43209
(614) 231-5364

Vienna Ice Cafe

viennaicecafe.com

2899 N High St
Columbus, OH 43202
(614) 268-3687

Johnson's Real Ice Cream

johnsonsrealicecream.com

2728 E Main St
Columbus, OH 43209
(614) 231-0014

Young's Jersey Dairy

youngsdairy.com

6880 Springfield Xenia Rd
Yellow Springs, OH 45387
(937) 325-0629

Vienna Ice

Vienna Ice Café, in the Clintonville neighborhood of Columbus, was started by two Austrians who wanted to bring the culture of Vienna abroad. With classical music, baked goods, and ice cream, Vienna Ice Café invites ice cream lovers for a respite with classic Vienna iced coffee.

viennaicecafe.com

2899 N High St

Columbus, OH 43202

(614) 268-3687

Any business—especially in food—is about bringing a dream and passions to life. Yet, starting a business is difficult, no matter where in the world it begins. In Europe, successful businesses build on centuries of familial relationships. New businesses struggle to gain credibility. "It's easier if you're born into it," Anand Saha laments about Europe.

But he and his wife Doris have succeeded with Vienna Ice Cafe and Mozart's, a dream from Europe. They met while working in five-star hotels in Switzerland where Doris studied pastry making, and Anand studied hotel management. When they wanted to start a business, moving to America was obvious, but they didn't want to lose the love of their home. For Anand and Doris, that meant bringing the traditions of Viennese food to America. Starting with Mozart's, a restaurant and bakery, Doris showcases her pastry making through Austrian classic treats, like the pastries from her childhood Austrian city of Mariazell. A natural choice for the restaurant's head chef, Doris emphasizes quality ingredients and artisanal methods. Mozart's may be in the United States, but the couple infuses the restaurant with European flair—classical music and traditional food. Because they found so much success in Columbus, they expanded to a shop two doors down to highlight Doris' gelato training. Vienna Ice Cafe highlights the pleasure of a classic Austrian cold dessert—the Vienna ice coffee and the shop's namesake.

After driving hours through rural Ohio, I arrive in the Clintonville neighborhood. In Mozart's, I sit with Anand at a table, adorned with white linen. Sunlight dances among the red and orange leaves on the trees shading the Ohio hills. Customers nibble on dishes of salads and baked goods. A black grand piano sits in a cozy corner, waiting to be played. "A quiche!" Anand insists and nods to a server across the room.

A slice of freshly baked quiche arrives on a plate surrounded by sliced bread and fruit salad. The quiche melts on my tongue. The egg custard flows between the flaky crust, black forest ham, and bacon.

Anand's language flows with accents from India and Austria. As we speak, Anand jumps up when he sees a familiar customer. A grin erupts across his face. Doris is at work in the back of the restaurant, hidden out of sight. Later, I find photos capturing her pride around her large decorated custom cakes. "She is the one with the quiet demeanor," Anand describes his wife.

We walk over to Vienna Ice Cafe. A cone with three pink scoops and the words "Vienna Ice Cafe: created by & crafted with everyone & everything you've always loved about Mozart's Cafe" is printed on a poster. *Willkommen*—a common greeting in German, the official language of Austria—headlines the poster. A large glass display case shows an array of flavors from traditional to novel. Each flavor reflects Doris' pastry chef experience in Europe. One tub holds chocolate truffle ice cream inspired by the chocolate truffle torte, a rich chocolate cake folded with baked hazelnuts and chocolate truffle frosting. Another holds Kahlua coffee, which tastes bold and earthy. Warm flavors like butter pecan and toffee beckon to be tried. A light green ice cream with chunks of key lime pie, the same pie in a display case at Mozart's. Another ice cream is folded with bits of tiramisu. "Unlike other shops, we do everything in house," Anand says. "We have the experience."

Because baked goods are made in house, the process is simple. At other shops, ice cream and gelato makers need to outsource their mix-ins, the ingredient that makes ice cream chunky—the broken cookie bits, fresh mascarpone, or candied orange peels. Here at Vienna Ice, those goods are freshly made at Mozart's. The flavors start with the basics like vanilla, strawberry, and chocolate, but they don't end there. "This allows us to have imagination," Anand adds. "We're going to try poppy seed rum raisin next."

He suggests "marzipan almond paste" as inspiration sparkles in his eyes. This may be a bakery lover's paradise, but I ask for the signature dish—the Vienna Ice Coffee. Dark coffee with scoops of vanilla ice cream is topped with whipped cream and shaved chocolate. Each bit of chocolate bursts with deep earthy flavor. In Vienna, locals order this coffee at least two times a week. It is the Viennese way.

Anand and Doris wanted to recreate a real Viennese cafe—a friendly place for children and adults. They imagined a place where people could socialize in a relaxed environment, surrounded by quality food. Ice cream is not served in paper cups. Rather, guests are encouraged to have ice cream in glass bowls. Fresh flowers infuse the air with their scent and brighten the room. The small marbled tables are close together, inviting patrons to crowd together around their bowls. It's a sit-down-and-socialize experience.

A fan writes in a guestbook:

Yumalicious so delicious

V - Very Good

I - interesting taste in my mouth

E - exhilarating

N - nothing like I ever tasted

N - no other place compares

A - awesome possum!

The ode to Vienna Ice Cafe is circled in blue vines. Just before this book's publication, Anand and Doris moved a few miles away to a bigger location, allowing them even more freedom to capture their vision of Europe.

"I redo what I like," Anand says. "I want to make it feel like I am coming home. Maybe people will ask, 'Are we in Vienna?'"

Young's Jersey Dairy

Young's Dairy Farm is a family destination in the town of Yellow Springs, near Dayton. Expanding beyond a dairy farm and ice cream shop, visitors can experience corn mazes, miniature golf, farm animals, and other farm activities.

youngsdairy.com

6880 Springfield Xenia Rd

Yellow Springs, OH 45387

(937) 325-0629

Americana means this: rolling roads passing through fields with wheat and sunflowers. White picket fences surround ranch houses. Bucolic scenes fill the drive from Columbus to Yellow Springs. The National Museum of the United States Air Force in Dayton, birthplace of aviation, lies several miles from here. I speed past rest stops, trees in autumn regalia, and small towns built around a single general store. Young's Jersey Dairy rises up at the side of the road as if beckoning a weary traveler.

A small windmill spins. A dollhouse replica Young's Jersey Dairy overlooks the miniature golf course. A fake cow perches on white sign with black lettering reading, "We create fun for our customers." Below that, a message advertises cornfield mazes for upcoming month of October. Later in the year, the sign changes to read, "Fresh strawberry milkshake" and "Try an apple dumpling a la mode." A green street sign declares a path in the parking lot, "Scoop-DeVille Lane." In a field, the cows moo. White baskets full of orange pumpkins line a fence like waiting toys. Wagons and tractors await passengers for rides. A child runs and hands a fistful of feed to a waiting goat.

A red barn lures me inside where wooden tables fill the room. A customer wears a t-shirt that says, "Around the world." He orders a root beer float and a vanilla shake from a young woman behind the ice cream dipping cabinet. A sign hangs on the wall, listing the available flavors. The walls are lined with pictures of ice cream delights from a bygone era—a hot fudge sundae for twenty cents, a strawberry cone for five cents, and a vanilla shake for ten cents.

Dan Young, the owner of Young's Jersey Dairy, calls himself the Chief Ice Cream Dipper. Better than President. Better than CEO. He plays with creation. "This is my favorite part of the job," he says, looking at the ice cream counter. "Folks are always in a good mood."

Dan is in his late fifties. Last week, he rode the Young's-sponsored

25-mile bike ride for charity. He wears a red jacket embroidered with his three-letter name in white. Whenever he speaks, he leans forward, gesturing with his fingers. Every few moments, a marketing idea crosses his mind, and he writes it down for a newly hired social media consultant. His background in retail and marketing from Miami University in Ohio enhances his business savvy—stretching beyond the initial ideas of the Young's Jersey Dairy. "I grew with the times," he says. "I thrived on chaos."

In 1896, relatives of the Young family built the red barn, which houses the primary activities of Young's Jersey Dairy. After World War II, Dan's grandfather purchased the nearby sixty acres in 1946. The Young family farmed the land and opened a tractor dealership. By the 1950s, the family sold milk to the public. The self-operated service operated successfully. On the porch, customers would leave change for the milk and would exchange an empty jug for a full jug. Within a decade, Dan's grandmother opened a retail store, selling milk, apples, and cheese. "It was like an early convenience store," Dan describes.

Then the city of Dayton asked the Young family a simple question: Can you make ice cream? The Young family explored that venture. "It can't be rocket science!" Dan says. "It was way cheaper to do homegrown ice cream."

Family members studied dairy science at Ohio State University in nearby Columbus, Ohio. The Young family stayed small, with focus on thirty-five flavors and limited cone types. Ice cream was made in small batches next to the red barn. By 1968, they began serving ice cream. Visitors began hearing of Young's Jersey Dairy through word of mouth. As they say, the rest is history.

Today, the red barn serves as a gathering place for communities like nonprofit organizations and nearby small towns. Young families, especially those from the nearby Patterson Air Force base, flock here

for a weekend destination.

Dan is curious. He wants to know what drives people, how the farm should be laid out, and what food people want to eat. In 1991, he added miniature golf course with a replica of the existing farm windmill. "Young's evolved to 'Create fun'," Dan says. "But ice cream is the number one thing."

Flavors matters for that value. Small children break into a run as they enter the Young's Jersey Dairy, where they sprint for the brightly-lit dipping cabinet containing over thirty flavors of ice cream and gelato. Classics like vanilla and strawberry are plentiful. But adventurous ice cream flavors can experiment with novelty flavors like "Cow Patty"—a dark chocolate ice cream folded with chocolate cookie pieces, chocolate-covered toffee pieces, and mini chocolate chips. Cincinnati inspired the ice cream flavor "Cayenne," a Tabasco-roasted chocolate ice cream. When Young's Jersey Dairy hosts an event, the team

concocts a specialty ice cream flavor. At a wool weavers gathering of 30,000 people, Dan and his colleagues imagined the flavor name "Wooly Wonka" to capture the excitement and diversity. Then they crafted the resulting flavor, a smooth caramel ice cream mixed with marshmallows and chocolate chunks. Seasons dictate changing flavors. Fall has arrived—pumpkin and cinnamon are highlights. Regardless of the season, the most popular flavor is chocolate peanut butter. In the late eighties, a young woman suggested a new flavor that attracts cookie lovers. Dan resisted, claiming its similarity to flavors like cookies & cream and flavors with cookie bits. She persisted, wanting to test this new flavor. "Quit pestering me," Dan recalls saying. He relented and produced the flavor. Within a few days, the flavor cookie dough ice cream sold out. "I learned to listen carefully to ideas," he says.

At 15% butterfat, the ice cream is rich, filling each lick with a creamy flavor. Behind a counter, assortments of cones are ready to be dipped in melted chocolate. A child orders the most popular combination—a chocolate dipped cone with chocolate peanut butter ice cream. The average customer? It's two dips of ice cream and one vanilla milkshake.

Outside next to the red barn, Dan guides me to a smaller building. Inside, workers churn ice cream in a standard ice cream machine, the same model that I have seen across the United States, but this one lacks modern buttons and switches. The "Emery Thompson" label is a faded blue. But age doesn't matter; the machine churns ice cream as effectively as new models. Next to the machine, white circular bins stand ready to catch the finished product. When completed, the workers push the bins through a shoulder-level door opening to a freezer. Peering through the door, I find a room of tubs containing finished ice cream.

"I want to listen between the lines," Dan says and dreams about what he can do next at Young's Jersey Dairy. "How about cheese?"

Goat Cheese Ice Cream with Carmelized Figs and Candied Bacon

Remove stems from figs. Quarter the stemmed figs into small chunks.

Mix figs, honey, a pinch of salt, juice of 1 lemon, water, liquor, and cinnamon stick in saucepan over high heat. Bring to a boil, then reduce heat to medium. Cook until the mixture has a sticky, jam-like consistency, around 30 minutes. Remove cinnamon stick. Let cool to room temperature. Set caramelized figs aside.

Preheat oven to 400 degrees.

Lay strips of bacon evenly on a baking sheet, covered with parchment paper or aluminum foil. Sprinkle generously 1-2 teaspoon of brown sugar evenly across each strip.

Place into oven and bake for approximately 7 minutes. Flip the bacon strips over and dredge them through the dark molasses collected on the baking sheet. Continue to bake until darkened, but not burnt, around 7 minutes. Remove from oven. Cool on wire rack or on paper towels to collect excess oil.

Chop or use a mini food processor to chop the candied bacon into small pieces. Set aside.

Combine cornstarch and 2 ½ tablespoons of the half and half in a small bowl. Mix, until there are no lumps, to create a cornstarch slurry.

In a separate large bowl, whisk goat cheese, and a pinch of salt until smooth.

Whisk the remaining half and half, sugar, and corn syrup in a saucepan set over medium heat. When the mixture begins to steam, add the cornstarch slurry. Continue to stir until the mixture thickens, about 1 minute. Gradually whisk the hot milk mixture into the goat cheese mixture until smooth.

Chill the mixture at least three hours or overnight in a refrigerator.

Scrape cold mixture into a pre-frozen ice-cream-maker bowl and churn according to manufacturer's instructions. Add chopped candied bacon five minutes before churning completes.

Scoop goat cheese ice cream into an empty resealable container. After every scoop, swirl in a generous spoonful of caramelized figs with a rubber spatula. Freeze up to a month. To serve, let stand at room temperature until slightly softened, about 10 minutes. Serve as is, or with fresh chopped or sliced figs.

Snowville Creamery: A Visit to a Dairy Plant

"Simplicity, patience, compassion. These three are your greatest treasures."

- Lao Tzu, *Tao Te Ching*

"Do you know what some people don't have?" Warren Taylor, the founder of a small dairy plant in Southeast Ohio, asks in between mouthfuls of garden-fresh Mediterranean salad and chicken bisteeya.

"Tongues!" he pounds the table, bouncing a basket of bread. "Some people don't know how to taste. I don't know why so many of us have forgotten how to taste. Rather, we eat what they tell us to eat."

For the next three hours, Warren's food philosophy punctuates every word, emphasizing his experience as founder and owner of the dairy plant, Snowville Creamery. His entrance into the restaurant was abrupt, waking up the hushed space, but diners recognized him and nodded as he strides toward the table. Warren is tall and lean. Warren's personality matches his gestures, always in motion. Upon arrival, his handshake literally shakes off any exhaustion from my two-hour drive from Columbus.

My story of meeting Warren begins several years ago, when I attended a film screening at a packed movie theater in downtown San Francisco. Upon seeing the words "food" and "free" in my email, I immediately signed up. The film begun, depicting a farmhouse outline, then zooming out to reveal a generic brand of butter. It zoomed out again, displays the rows of shelves in an American grocery store. After watching *Food, Inc.*, I mumbled to a friend, "I don't know if I believe it."

Did I see the truth about something that I enjoyed everyday? For months afterward, I only ate organic and local, asked "is this organic?" like the quintessential San Franciscan, shopped at farmers markets, and avoided fast food chains like McDonald's and KFC. This kind of food budget was not sustainable. As time passed, I reverted back to buying conventionally grown foods. However, my eating habits changed, and my lifestyle focused on home-cooked food. Having dinner with others became important to me. Because of my sensitivity to bitter tastes, I still hated eating greens, but I discovered the pleasure of growing plants and cooking foods from scratch.

As Warren speaks, the same thoughts after watching *Food, Inc.* rush through my mind. Was this what ice cream was about? It seems that bubblegum ice cream, my favorite flavor in childhood, was nothing more than a marketing novelty (bright blue, red, pink, yellow gumballs in ice cream)! During my research, many ice cream makers lamented how real mint ice cream scared customers—"This is mint? Why doesn't it taste like mint in Dreyer's? Why does it taste like toothpaste? Why isn't it bright green? Why can't ice cream be like the ice cream I grew up with!"

So many ice cream lovers have forgotten what ice cream used to be like.

I wanted to know the people behind the ice cream, but discovered that ice cream makers were just the first layer. By this point, I had interviewed the owners of fifteen shops, and I was still struggling to understand what ice cream was about. I had expected to find artisanal ice cream makers mixing milk, cream, and sugar like I did in my home kitchen when following their cookbooks. To my surprise, that was not the case. "Big Dairy", as many called it, had significant impact on them—the ice cream shops struggled with exorbitant fees for health inspections and confusing laws from the dairy industry. A few ice cream makers were secretive, protective of their dairy sources. Even after assuring one maker of my confidence, he gestured to his ice cream, "What you see here is what you get." Another shamelessly showed me prefab plastic bags containing an ice cream base (made of the essentials to ice cream: cream, milk, and sugar) soon to be combined with peach syrup from a large can. "Every ice cream shop in the city uses the same mix," she revealed. "How can anyone afford to make their own?" Another maker proudly displayed cans of syrup imported from Italy. He was proud that he planned to mix chocolate and strawberry puree to make strawberry chocolate ice cream—"a crazy combination for the strawberry and chocolate lovers!" I was troubled that the ingredients were not whole—which was the original way of making ice cream. In my research, I found few ice cream shops that cut up their own fruit and created custom ice cream bases.

Jeni's Splendid Ice Cream was different. On the website of Jeni's—the most notable local chain of ice cream shops in Columbus—I discovered Snowville Creamery as their preferred source for dairy. Jeni's Splendid Ice Cream has a direct relationship with Snowville Creamery, which produces a custom dairy mix for the popular ice cream shop. So I called for an interview. I wanted to understand what made Warren Taylor and his dairy plant different. Over the phone with Warren, I asked about their dairy farms. He launched into a brief story of his work in dairy science at a Safeway in Northern California, and the inspiration to start a small, efficient creamery in Ohio, his home state and where he studied dairy technology in college. He boomed, "To get the best experience of Snowville Creamery, you should be here early in the morning. We have an extra room in the back of the house. Stay the night."

"No wine?" he notices my empty glass and waves over a server. "After your long drive, you must have wine!"

I smile. Just twenty minutes ago, I had arrived before he did, and the server insisted on an immediate answer to Warren's very important question for me—*red or white?* I thank him for the offer.

"I'll have a glass of beer," he says when the server arrives. "Oh, and I always pray before a meal."

He orders the best dishes, insisting on introducing me to the dishes he and his family have enjoyed. I tell him about what I want to discover at Snowville. I sense that he has a lot of thoughts to share, and I sit back to listen.

To nobody in particular, he asks aloud, "Why do people eat together?"

Then in a few moments, he looks at me and answers, "To share. We are doing that. We are doing what so many forget."

I nod as I tear a piece from the bread.

Large, colorful tapestries adorn the interior of Restaurant Salaam. The Mediterranean restaurant where I am meeting Warren for the first time is in Athens, Ohio, twenty-four miles from Snowville Creamery. Intricate patterns of green and yellow flowers on a blue sea of tablecloth cover each small table, where diners lean forward in quiet conversation. Large family-style platters filled with fresh mint, grapes, and almonds sit on many of the tables as the aroma of sautéed ground lamb and freshly baked, layered pastries fill the air. The restaurant owners grow produce in their garden and use dairy from Warren's creamery. I have no trouble believing that Warren knows Restaurant Salaam well. We both indulge in savory chicken pastry and vegan spicy coconut curry.

"There's a Chinese saying that goes, 'If you're hungry, feed your parents.'" Warren says. "It's Confucian filial piety. It's a sign of respect to the people who came before you."

Remembering past practices is important, especially when it comes to dairy. With every poignant remark about food, he relates his beliefs to Tai Chi, describing how it transforms his everyday life. Peering from his glasses under his graying hair, his gaze swallows everything around us—the blue walls in the restaurant, the smiles from familiar townspeople, and the glass of beer, shaking with every fervent remark. Dressed in a simple plaid button-down shirt, he talks to me like a protégé, dishing out lines of wisdom.

"Did you know that there are only two foods created by nature? That is, the only two foods created by animals just for a source of food? Milk and honey. That's it."

As I discover later, Warren is correct. Nuts, leaves, and eggs are

made for other purposes—fertilization or energy storage. He is referring to abundance much like the Bible's expression of an abundant land—"a land flowing of milk and honey".

At his house near the dairy plant, Warren's wife greets us in the open kitchen, tugging at the long rope holding back two large, wolf-like dogs. I am surprised by the dogs' size, but push myself in, offering a gift of tea for their hospitality. Her long graying hair swings to frame her face as we share a cup together. Their daughter, home from working with a cheesemaker, sits near the large windows. She looks tired, comfortable with the shrouded darkness outside that is broken by dots of light from neighboring houses miles away. Another dog with scraggly fur patters across the hardwood floors. I ask about a wooden carving of a male face above the food pantry. It appears to be growing out of the wall, and its gaze is omniscient.

"The Green Man," Warren says. "My Filipino friend and I walked through the woods until he found a log that brought him to tears. The log spoke to him, telling him that there's something special in the land. I took that log, and he carved faces for me."

In the morning, Warren's truck carries us forward through the Ohio countryside toward Snowville Creamery in Pomeroy. With the land brightly lit, a nearby city rises up like an oasis. Dirt roads cross the rolling fields, which shimmer like fresh green paint. Warren says, "This county is one of the poorest in Ohio, because the land isn't great for growing. The soil is thin with a layer of red clay and grass. But it's great for cows. Because they don't need the land to be flat!"

We speed forward, kicking up a trail of dust. Warren adds, "We are farming grass! You know, cows are smart. They eat just enough. Not more, not less."

Arriving at the creamery, Warren points out the dairy farm owned by Bill Dix and Stacy Hall where cows wait to be milked. The cows crowd forward, eager to be rid of the heavy weight of milk. Once finished, the cows amble out of the building in a single line toward an open pasture. Warren says, "You can tell when a cow is not doing well by the way she walks. Look at that one."

One cow, the last one in the line, colored with patches of cream and brown, limps on her rear left leg.

"A confined animal is a stupid animal," Warren says. "Bill and Stacy want the cows to be happy. The emotional state affects their blood and in turn the milk."

The milk goes directly into the neighboring dairy plant. Inside, metal vats and pipes fill the small space. We climb to the top floor where he explains his philosophy of efficiency and sustainability. He built the dairy plant to be compact, taking advantage of gravity (building containers up high and letting gravity pull down the mixture) and moving all equipment (pasteurizer, centrifuge) close together. Unlike his previous dairy plants in California, the plant at Snowville Creamery is a well-oiled machine—no motion is wasted and very much like Warren himself. Even the water used to spray down the plant is returned to the land as irrigation. As we step on the planks above the machines, Warren says, "Most dairy plants are done by architects that do not understand what a dairy plant really needs. When I built this, 6,000 square feet was available, but I only planned for 600 square feet to process the milk. A small capacity facility leads to high levels of efficiency."

Warren boasts, "Only five people in the world think this way. Myself and four other dairy technologists."

On posters in the office, a milkmaid pouring milk from a jug is drawn against a grassy field. Standing near the milk lab, Warren brings out samples of fresh milk—chocolate milk, whole milk, low-fat milk, nonfat milk, heavy cream, and the ice cream base custom-made for Jeni's Splendid Ice Cream. The milk is pasteurized at a lower heat than most milk to maintain freshness. They are stored in paper cartons to protect any degradation from light.

"You must take a sip, let it warm up in your mouth, and then swallow. See how it's clean? It leaves a clean aftertaste." As he takes a taste of the milk, he smiles. "That's good."

The milk is filling and satisfying, reminiscent of the warm milk I drank in the mornings before school. It is sweet, and I want more.

His energy surges again, and he says, "You know, initially our milk was targeted to the upper class—families with median incomes of 150k. But then we were surprised. Families who made somewhere between 40k to 50k kept buying the milk. They know how to taste. You see!"

His voice echoes in the space, breaking the silence. Warren laughs, a booming sound that causes his colleagues to chuckle. Above the entrance to the offices, another Green Man hangs quietly. He nods and says, "Yes, he also is here."

Before I head back to Columbus, Warren looks at his bookshelf and finds a copy of Lao Tzu's *Tao Te Ching* (meaning "The Classic of the Way and Its Virtue"). He carries extra copies in case he meets someone worthy of the gift. Then he sautés slices of foraged mushrooms and gives me a jar of fresh yogurt and berries. Dodging construction and driving through the bucolic hills, with the book on Taoist philosophy lying in the backseat, I drink the mixture and relish the freshness and love of homemade food.

5

New York City

Romantic comedies set in New York City begin with a monologue describing the love of the city. The beauty lies in crowded subways, honking taxis, brutal weather, diverse food, and a hurried pace of living. No matter where I travel, I hear: "I want to visit New York." To many, this city represents America. "Live in New York once" is repeated advice from current and former New Yorkers.

To me, New York City represents the urban paradise, radiating with energy. I have this childhood memory: a concrete jungle of complex navigation; we climbed the Statue of Liberty, gazed out from the top of the Empire State Building, and roamed Chinatown looking for restaurants.

For residents, that is not New York. During an interlude as an East Coast resident, I understood the truth. As I drove (unintentionally) through Times Square, impatient pedestrians spilled through the streets, challenging my California-grown driving. I tensed. In the backseat, my Staten Island friend said, "Just mow them over. They will understand." Everyone is going somewhere. I learned to pop out by subway at Times Square, to sample desserts without guilt, and to sit on your own stoop drinking coffee.

Food brings people together—whether by historical legends or innovation. In New York, it's the cronut, a croissant-doughnut pastry at Dominique Ansel Bakery. Or perhaps the classic pastrami sandwich at Katz's Delicatessen. Or perhaps it's the New York style pizza, a meal that busy locals swear by. Or the breakfast of bagels and lox. Then the ice cream shops—the one that stock city-grown pints to be eaten in cramped apartments, the one with a sister shop in central Africa that aims to empower working women, or the one serving ice cream laced with floral notes from a yellow food truck. The stories are rich here in this grand city.

Big Gay Ice Cream Shop

biggayicecream.com

125 E 7th St
  New York, NY 10009
  (212) 533-9333
125 E 7th St
  New York, NY 10009
  (212) 533-9333

Victory Garden

victorygardennyc.com

31 Carmine St
  New York, NY 10014
  (212) 206-7273

The Original Chinatown Ice Cream Factory

chinatownicecreamfactory.com

65 Bayard St
  New York, NY 10013
  (212) 608-4170

Van Leeuwen Artisan Ice Cream

vanleeuwenicecream.com

Food truck roving location and hours

48 E 7th St
  New York, NY 10003
  (718) 715-0758
620 Manhattan Ave
  Brooklyn, NY 11222
  (347) 987-4774
81 Bergen St
  Brooklyn, NY 11201
  (347) 763-2979

Blue Marble Ice Cream

bluemarbleicecream.com

196 Court St
  Brooklyn, NY 11201
  (347) 384-2100
186 Underhill Ave
  Brooklyn, NY 11238
  (718) 399-6926

Ample Hills Creamery

amplehills.com

623 Vanderbilt Ave
  Brooklyn, NY 11238
  (347) 240-3926

Victory Garden

Victory Garden, located in the cozy West Village, formed on the basis that "ice cream wasn't a sin". Made from goat milk and crafted by a former nutritionist, the soft serve is inspired by Turkish ice cream.

victorygardennyc.com

31 Carmine St

New York, NY 10014

(212) 206-7273

"Victory Garden Herbal Blend," Sophia Brittan names the herbal goat milk soft serve flavor. "It captures the summer. That best represents Victory Garden."

This flavor is both the shop's namesake and best represents the shop's essence. Made from ingredients from local markets, Victory Garden Herbal Blend incorporates herbs like rosemary, sage, mint, lemon thyme, anise, cardamom, and orange blossom. The owner, Sophia Brittan, muses that the flavor "captures the multi-palate society" and Mediterranean cuisine. With ingredients sourced from local purveyors and using goat milk for the base, Victory Garden aims to make soft serve for everyone. When she says everyone, she means *everyone*. People who are lactose intolerant can have goat milk. "I wanted to make something that wasn't a sin," Sophia says.

After studying holistic nutrition, Sophia wanted to create something meaningful. It was 2007, and Sophia felt isolated from working at home. Watching online cooking shows, she became inspired. She remembered the unique flavor of goat milk. Experimenting, she combined goat milk and Greek yogurt, and then mixed the result with pomegranate seeds and walnuts. "I never tasted anything like that," she recalls.

From that taste, she began creating soft serve ice cream. Harnessing local produce, she began testing. Goat milk was the key, a flavor that was similar to skim milk but carried the rich qualities of the well-loved ice cream. For many, goat milk is easier to digest than cow milk. She observed that many believed that ice cream is indulgent and frozen yogurt is healthy. "Because when people hear yogurt, they think 0 fat and 0 calories," Sophia says.

But still ice cream is ice cream. It must contain fat and some sugar to make it ice cream. It cannot achieve the right density without those components. As a child, Sophia frequented Tasti-D-Lite, which serves soft serve. What if a dessert could combine quality foods and ice cream together, she thought. She loved soft serve, but wanted something natural. A dessert that used local produce and included holistic nutritional values. She wanted a food that went beyond dessert. So Sophia explored options.

Her excitement grows as she describes her international travel, the source of inspiration for Victory Garden. In Lebanon and Egypt, she indulged in soft serve that was more refreshing than its counterpart in America. While traveling abroad in Turkey, she tasted the Middle Eastern ice cream, *dondurma*, which had a delicate taste enhanced by salep, a wild orchid found only in Turkey. The *dondurma* stretched easily and could be eaten with a fork and knife. Sophia noticed an opportunity—nobody had interpreted *dondurma* for American tastes. Soon, the concept of Victory Garden was born.

While seeking the perfect location in the competitive market of New

York City, Sophia tested proposed flavors. This extra time allowed for iteration and self-education. She taste-tested the soft serve with herself, friends, and colleagues. Sophia limited the number of ingredients. As we sit near the front display window, she smiles as she recalls the shop history, "I learned: don't get too crazy. Keep it simple."

When she opened Victory Garden, she knew that chocolate, lemon poppy, orange blossom, and salted caramel must be featured flavors. Then a Mexican man, her seller of goat milk, suggested Victory Garden's current popular flavor: caramel. Its sweet and savory flavor profile attracted fans.

The initial reactions to goat milk were skeptical. Visitors assumed that the store would carry jugs of goat milk, yet it did not. The soft serve differed from typical soft serve in the states. Yet once customers taste it, they understand—the soft serve is tangy and flavorful. Customers understand that flavors reflect the season. Victory Garden become part of some customers' routine, stopping by for the soft serve once a week.

Located in the West Village neighborhood in Manhattan, Victory Garden beckons passersby with a cozy environment—hanging plants frames a white interior, and clover leaves décor dance on the walls. Outside, an older lady rests on a wide bench. She glances inside, studying the abundance of selections. Near the entrance, daily flavors written on a chalkboard range from tangy goat milk and salted caramel to dates and yogurt. Other desserts like mini goat cheesecakes and yogurt are available.

Inside, Katy Perry plays on the loudspeakers, and the pop beat adds color to the white counters. Exposed brick suggests the homegrown quality of the shop. Smooth white pots of plants frame the floor to ceiling window. On the wall, descriptions declare the soft serve's benefits from taste, "deliciously sweet and earthy," to nutrition, "a great source of iron, calcium, protein, and potassium." On another wall, a tall photo displays goats circling a white statue. Every few minutes, a customer wanders in from the street. A Victory Garden staff member pulls a lever, and the soft serve machine rumbles to life, keeping the frozen delight churned and ready.

Like the shop's namesake flavor, Sophia aims to make flavors with deep meaning. She loves the tangy flavor of Greek yogurt and the natural floral taste of goat milk. Using those base tastes, she balances the flavors. Sophia made "The Healing Powers of India," a warm flavor combining turmeric and ginger—those herbs serve as the base of fall stews. Or, "yoga-ish" as she calls it. For another flavor, she enlivened chocolate with rosemary, her favorite chocolate combination at Victory Garden. Another flavor combines dates and yogurt. Honoring her Turkish inspiration, she plays with walnuts and pomegranates. In the summer, she looks forward to experimenting with watermelon, orange blossom, and black currant. Fruit flavors offer opportunity to experiment. "It's always interesting how people want to ask for flavors that are common here in June in the month of January," she says. "It's hard to explain the seasonality."

In the back, Sophia experiments with a new chocolate flavor—something that could work for vegans and others who needed a special diet. Carob. She is in her late twenties, and tortoise shell eyeglasses frame her eyes. A gray handkerchief, printed with turquoise clover leaves, covers her hair. Like her staff, she wears a white v-neck t-shirt printed with the Victory Garden logo—a goat's head where one half is a turquoise opaque shadow and the other half is an outline of floral plants. Sophia pulls out a paper cup and gets a sample of goat milk soft serve from the machine. Tasting it, she smiles. "Perfect," she says.

Outside, at the bottom of Victory Garden's sidewalk chalkboard, "Enjoy! Repeat tomorrow!" is written next to a pink hand-drawn heart around the words: "Feel Good."

The Original Chinatown Ice Cream Factory

Chinatown Ice Cream Factory broke through challenging economic times in the 1970s by opening an ice cream shop. Now primarily run by the owner's daughter, the ice cream boasts classic flavors and exotic Chinese flavors like lychee and green tea.

chinatownicecreamfactory.com

65 Bayard St

New York, NY 10013

(212) 608-4170

In between large businesses, a green dragon with a toothy smile holds a bowl of white-colored ice cream. Vanilla, obviously. I correct myself: I am in Manhattan's Chinatown. Printed Chinese characters accompany English words on signs. Mandarin and Cantonese dialects float down the sidewalks. The dragon is highly revered, considered lucky and powerful. And the white ice cream? Likely lychee, coconut, or another Asian-influenced flavor.

Chinatown Ice Cream Factory is small. Its narrow space, dominated by the display case, invites customers to ogle the flavors. Flattened decorative crepe paper dances along the walls. In the back, out of sight, chocolate fudge ice cream churns. An employee places a tub of cantaloupe ice cream into position. He makes eye contact with customers and asks, "May I help you, ladies?" With no chairs inside, customers take their scoops to nearby Columbus Park to enjoy and people watch.

It's early evening. Older Chinese ladies rush to pick up pre-ordered ice cream cakes. Their voices increase the volume to a lively pitch. As they gossip, they squeeze together by a refrigerated case holding ice cream cakes shaped like hearts and circles. More than one hundred cakes are made daily.

Christina Seid sits behind the display case and helps the ladies. The shop is not closing soon. The shop is open for twelve hours for customers, but Christina works before opening hours and beyond closing hours. The weekend bustle may demand more of her time. Outside, New York City changes rapidly. Inside, the shop's character has stayed the same for decades.

In the late 1970s, Christina's father Philip opened Chinatown Ice Cream Factory. Back then Chinatown consisted of a few blocks. It was the year of the snake, an animal of the Chinese zodiac. Originally he planned for a sandwich shop, but the demand for sandwiches did not exist. Noticing a lack of dessert in the neighborhood, he switched to ice cream, despite its high cost of ingredients and process. Christina's grandmother supported Philip and experimented with flavors like red bean, lychee, green tea, and mango. Knowing that the Chinese preferred subtle flavors, they developed ice cream that appealed to the Chinatown locals.

"Everything was so strange to non-Chinese people who asked 'What is green tea? What is mango?'" Christina says. "But it appealed to the Chinese people."

The shop was a success. Non-Chinese visitors hesitated at green tea and mango flavors, but the Chinese locals embraced these familiar flavors. Slowly, the shop garnered a following from all visitors.

Having grown up in the Little Neck neighborhood in Queens, Christina never intended to work in ice cream. The Seid family had a limited income, but Philip promised his children: "If you work hard, you don't have to work here. You can go to school and get a desk job."

Christina did that. Intending to work as a teacher, she studied education. Yet during school breaks like on the weekends and evenings, Christina worked at the ice cream shop. Her desire to teach waned, and her appreciation for the family business grew. Christina realized that her energy could only be dedicated to one thing—teaching or ice cream. So she chose ice cream and partnered with her father as a co-owner. "Entrepreneurship started becoming cool and accepted," Christina explains. "It's weird that it became cool, because it wasn't always a cool thing. Not cool, like before, working for your dad. But now I love it."

Christina and Philip guide the vision of Chinatown Ice Cream Factory. They established a working style that complements one another's skills. "When you get older, you develop a bond with your parents with the type of work you do. It makes you appreciate your parents."

Christina experiments with ice cream, which is made in the back of the shop. Guided by a demand for unique flavors, she played with chocolate bacon ice cream. Playing with Asian cultures, she created "Zen Butter," an Asian take on the banana ice cream with fudge and walnuts of Ben & Jerry's Chunky Monkey. Inspired by the nutty flavors of sesame noodles, she created this Asian spin-off with peanut butter ice cream and toasted sesame seeds. The black sesame and spicy wasabi flavors, Christina boasts, are inspired by Asian tastes. She is proud of the pandan ice cream, made with leaves found in Southeast Asian cooking. On my tongue, the green-colored ice cream melts into a nutty, minty finish. "It would be good to introduce Chinese flavors to non-Chinese people and vice versa like pumpkin pie," she says. "The best way to introduce cultures is by food because everyone has to eat. "

Curious about ice cream elsewhere, she looked abroad, especially Italy. She mapped out the gelato shops and visited them. "I learned from Rome that gelato is to be eaten in moderation," she recalls her trip. "I prefer ice cream. Ice cream is tastier. It is a mainstay in America for a reason."

The trip to Italy confirmed for Christina that she loves ice cream: nothing is as rich and dense in every lick. Gelato was not the same. Christina's favorite ice cream is still at Chinatown Ice Cream Factory. While pregnant, she consumed tubs of ice cream. In a moment when she was out, her husband purchased premium ice cream from a nearby grocery store. After one scoop, she tossed it out, because it did not meet her standards.

Today, Chinatown Ice Cream Factory is an institution in New York City. The shop is a popular stop on food tours. Local schools help design the shop's awnings and banners. Marriage proposals and scavenger hunts are common occurrences. Christina remembers a non-Chinese couple that proposed in the shop, because it was the location of their first date. The shop changed a flavor to "Will you marry me?" at the boyfriend's request. "To be part of big moments in people's lives is good, even if it's in an indirect way," Christina says. "It's dessert that makes people happy."

Christina is proud of the ice cream's status. She gestures to the "boasting wall," a wall adorned with red and gold Chinese decorations. The decorations surround media clippings full of accolades for the shop, such as the *Village Voice* newspaper and the Citysearch online guide. During Hurricane Sandy, the shop lost all of its ice cream during the power outages. The day that power returned, a writer from the Louis Vuitton guide visited Chinatown Ice Cream Factory, cementing their ice cream as a high-end dessert.

"The lychee flavor is our staple flavor," she says, glancing at the display case. "It's the one we sell the most. People ask if we are scared of Coldstone. Froyo comes and goes. Everyone is trying to be like everyone else. Well, our lychee flavor has been selling for thirty years. Chinatown Ice Cream Factory is delicious and decently priced. That's why we have long lines. We broke through all cultural barriers. We stayed with who we are."

Van Leeuwen

Van Leeuwen started as the first artisanal food trucks roaming through New York City and eventually opened storefronts in Brooklyn and Manhattan. The founding trio aims to let fresh ingredients speak through ice cream flavors like vanilla and palm sugar.

vanleeuwenicecream.com

Food truck roving location and hours

48 E 7th St

New York, NY 10003

(718) 715-0758

620 Manhattan Ave

Brooklyn, NY 11222

(347) 987-4774

81 Bergen St

Brooklyn, NY 11201

(347) 763-2979

In Brooklyn, a buttery yellow food truck waits on Bedford Avenue. Outlined in white script, the letters "Van Leeuwen" grace the passenger door. Like a page of pressed flowers, hand-sketched plants accompany ice cream flavors in flowing script on the menu. The words "Palm Sugar" and a description of its origin from palm sap display across two hand-drawn palm trees. Cacao nuts and leaves circle the word "Chocolate." The window begins at the customer's counter height, no need tiptoeing here. The window, "approachable and easy to work in" as the founders describe, opens wider than a typical food truck, revealing ice cream freezers and other glistening equipment.

Hipsters, dressed in tight jeans and black-framed glasses, saunter by and pause to study the menu. From within the truck, a woman smiles. The customers hand the woman a few dollars, and she turns to scoop ice cream hidden in a humming freezer. Her red hair is twisted and pulled backward with a blue handkerchief.

I choose vanilla, the flavor prized for its complex mixture of two vanilla beans, hailing from Madagascar's Bourbon region and the Islands of Tahiti. The woman leans through the window, which starts at her knees, to hand me the cone. The vanilla ice cream is familiar and delicate. Specks of vanilla bean appear throughout the ice cream. "What would you like?" says the woman to the next customer.

Much like the food trucks, the Van Leeuwen ice cream shops embody the same space design. Outside the first brick and mortar Van Leeuwen shop in Greenpoint, a book titled New York Day Hikes, lies on a weathered bench. My sister examines it and brings it inside. The girl with a pixie-cut haircut behind the Van Leeuwen counter raises her eyebrows and says, "I know who left it outside. He leaves it hoping someone will pick it up."

Framed by green potted plants, the open windows of the Greenpoint store provide a literal window into the neighborhood. Once dominated by Polish immigrants, the neighborhood is gentrifying. Across the street, a tired pink building housing Baskin Robbins stands. Buttery yellow accents the Van Leeuwen shop—framing the hanging shop sign, circling a wooden banner, and dancing across the white tin foil ceiling. Behind the counter, the girl exchanges French with customers. A woman in dark blue jeans saunters into the shop and exclaims that it's "a beautiful day to ride a bike." She orders an iced mocha and mango chili sorbet. Coins clatter into the tip jar. Independent rock music floats from old-style mounted speakers with male voices intermingling with crashing cymbals. Then the vinyl record changes. The Supremes sing, their voices dancing among the marble tables and wooden chairs.

My sister and I slowly devour a cup of pistachio ice cream, letting the nutty flavor float across our tongues then linger as the cream falls down our throats. The pistachios, grown on Mt. Etna in Italy, are the most expensive to produce. The nuts are grown for a year, then

harvested and grounded to a light green paste. On one wall, a black and white drawing of a food truck seems to hang in the air, held up by pink, yellow, and blue balloons. A string of summertime flags frames the sketch by the owners' friend Joanna. Brass knobs, black walnut, and marble reflect the shop's former life as a bar.

Laura O'Neill and her two partners formed the ice cream business. Inspired by Good Humor trucks, the Van Leeuwen brothers Ben and Peter, Laura's two partners, set out to build an ice cream business. Meeting Ben in London while studying abroad, Laura joined the two. Starting with the food trucks, they honored the ice cream trucks of their childhood, remembering the animal-shaped popsicles and multi-layered ice rocket ships. Yet as they became familiar with the culinary world, the brothers learned that their childhood favorites lacked quality ingredients. Rather, it was industrialized, and artificially flavored. The three wanted to create a welcoming experience like childhood ice cream trucks, but serve food reflecting homegrown values and natural ingredients. Like the Good Humor trucks, they wanted to build a lasting institution, which gave back to the community. In 2008, the trucks began dotting the New York City landscape with their yellow colors brightening the streets. Starting in Soho and Brooklyn, they lured passersby. "I never knew that the first day could attract so many people," Laura remembers.

Laura drives an official Van Leeuwen black truck and parks right in front of the Greenpoint store. Running into the shop in a summer dress, she plops herself across from me and describes her hectic day managing the six food trucks. "The trucks can be a pain in the ass like a flat tire or battery issue," she says. "Anything that can go wrong, goes wrong."

As a former event planner, Laura knows the risks of running a business—market growth, financial gain, and employees. Yet the reward of authenticity propelled the three to success. After the trucks, they opened shops, sold at festivals, and stocked pints in Whole Foods, next to established ice cream brands. "The trucks, as cool as they are, aren't permanent, but a store here is pretty amazing to be in this neighborhood," Laura says.

Laura's descriptions are delivered with an accent from her home country, Australia. It sounds rough, like she's ready to take me on an

adventure. Smiling, she describes the origins of the flavors: the sugar from a coconut tree tapped in Bali, the purity of the chocolate, and the hand-selected California strawberries. She misses passion fruit, a common fruit in Australia. No stabilizers are present in the ice cream. Each spoonful has 22% butterfat, resulting in a creamy texture. A recent business venture, Selamat Pagi, a Balinese restaurant, extends their values to a full dining experience. The restaurant serves Van Leeuwen black sticky rice ice cream for dessert. Laura manages public relations and marketing. Pete focuses on the truck management, and Ben works on the recipes. Laura remembers as a child having frozen bananas on a stick, inspiring the roasted banana ice cream, which tastes like banana bread pudding. "We started with the classics," Laura says. "We wanted to do what made sense with the ice cream. Each flavor is a celebration of one ingredient. Like the Earl Grey ice cream is a sweet cup of tea."

Flavors at Van Leeuwen now number in the thirties, but twelve flavors are core to Van Leeuwen Artisan Ice Cream. More flavors are produced for the holidays and seasons. A chili ice cream celebrates Cinco de Mayo. Recipes are inspired by Thomas Keller's recipes and David Lebovitz's ice cream recipe book, *The Perfect Scoop*. They experiment and toss when the flavors do not work. A fifteen-gallon tank pasteurizes their ice cream base. Vegan ice cream is a growing point of pride for Van Leeuwen, answering requests from customers with dietary restrictions. They use the natural thickener guar gum to make sure the vegan ice cream remains a close cousin of its dairy equivalent. "We never compromise on quality ever," Laura says. "Companies cut corners, but we are at the core of our company and our product."

Celery Ice Cream with Peanut Butter Swirl and Rum-Soaked Raisins

Combine ½ cup granulated sugar with water and rum in a small saucepan. Boil and stir often, until sugar dissolves. Pour syrup over raisins in a medium bowl. Set aside. When ready for use, drain the mixture.

Whisk peanut butter with heavy cream, corn syrup and brown sugar in a small saucepan set over low heat. Continue whisking until sugar dissolves. Let cool to room temperature. Set aside.

Stir half and half with 1 cup granulated sugar in a medium saucepan over medium heat, until mixture starts to steam and bubbles start to form at sides of pan. Remove from heat and add celery. Steep for at least an hour.

Strain and discard celery. Stir in celery salt. Warm celery cream in same saucepan over medium heat until it starts to steam.

Whisk egg yolks in a large bowl. Wrap a damp kitchen towel around the base of the bowl (to prevent it from slipping). Gradually whisk in half of hot cream mixture. Return entire mixture to saucepan set over medium-low heat. Stir with wooden spoon constantly, until mixture is thick enough to coat the back of the spoon. Pour through a fine sieve into a metal bowl. Let stand for 10 min. Then lay plastic wrap directly on surface to prevent skin from forming.

Chill for at least three hours or overnight in the refrigerator. Scrape cold mixture into a pre-frozen ice-cream-maker bowl and churn according to manufacturer's instructions. Add rum-plumped raisins five minutes before churning completes.

Scoop celery ice cream into an empty resealable container. After every scoop, swirl in a generous spoonful of peanut butter sauce with a rubber spatula. Freeze up to a month. To serve, let stand at room temperature until slightly softened, about 10 minutes.

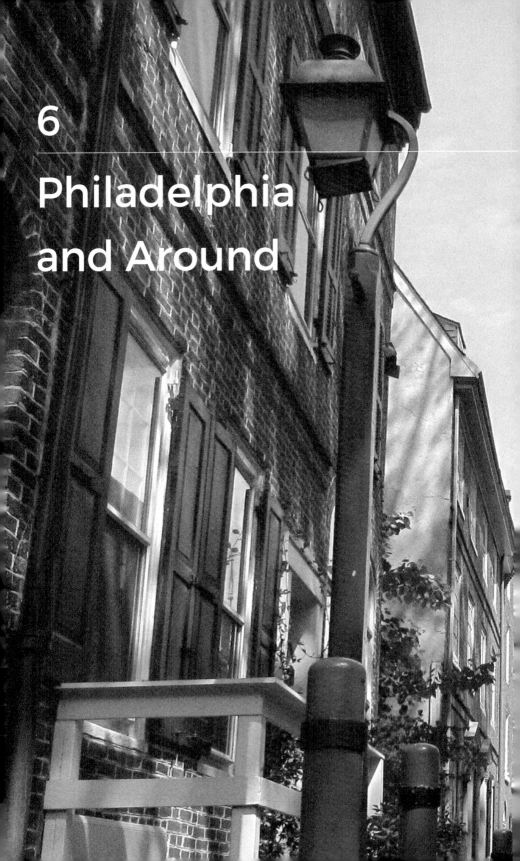

6

Philadelphia and Around

History is omnipresent in Philadelphia, nicknamed the "Cradle of Liberty" and "City of Brotherly Love." The city served as the nation's capitol not once, but twice—first during the American Revolutionary War and second while Washington D.C. was built. Within a square mile, one finds the buildings touched by the Declaration of Independence and meeting places for the Founding Fathers of the United States. Lines snake to visit the classic architecture and symbolic relics. At 239 Arch Street, a colonial-era building housed Betsy Ross as she sewed the first American flag. Plaques declare the locations of interest. History happened here—more three hundred years ago in the 1700s.

Today, the city is well known for heart-pumping Philly cheesesteaks and the Rocky montage ending at the top of 72 stone steps. But unique moments exist. Locals revel in the New Year's Mummers Parade, where groups march in costumes for satire, theater, and handiwork bragging rights. Known as Philadelphia's Magic Gardens, empty glass bottles, old bicycle wheels, and broken tiles decorate a sunny space. Food recalls tradition like the handcrafted Italian pulled pork sandwich and a summer treat at Pop's Homemade Water Ice.

When I embarked on this journey, I asked ice cream shop owners about the eggless ice cream base: "Is Philadelphia style invented in Philadelphia?" Many nodded, but could not pinpoint its origin. Like the United States, ice cream's greatest moments happened in or near Philadelphia—the invention of a hand-cranked machine by Nancy Johnson in 1843, the increasing popularity of ice cream among the American elite like George Washington, and the Breyers brand ice cream founding.

Here one finds ice cream from a multiple-generation family, a nostalgic ice cream parlor, and a classic dairy farm. The greatness of Philadelphia-style ice cream lies in the purity of its form—milk, sugar, and cream. That's the best ice cream possible.

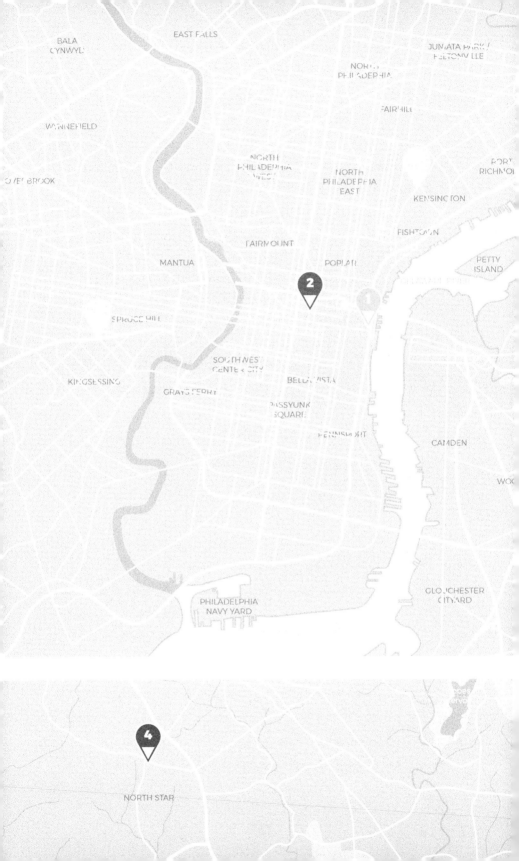

 ### Franklin Fountain

franklinfountain.com

116 Market St

Philadelphia, PA 19106

(215) 627-1899

 ### Bassett's Ice Cream

bassettsicecream.com

45 N 12th St

Philadelphia, PA 19107

(215) 925-4315

Little Baby's Ice Cream

littlebabysicecream.com

4903 Catharine St

Philadelphia, PA 19143

(215) 921-2100

2311 Frankford Ave

Philadelphia, PA 19125

(267) 687-8567

 ### Woodside Farm Creamery

woodsidefarmcreamery.com

1310 Little Baltimore Rd

Hockessin, DE 19707

(302) 239-9847

Franklin Fountain

Franklin Fountain captures the old-style ice cream parlor and soda fountain. Coming from an antique-collecting family, two brothers opened Franklin Fountain to capture a long-past era of ice cream sodas and old-fashioned candies.

franklinfountain.com

116 Market St

Philadelphia, PA 19106

(215) 627-1899

Nostalgia reigns in The Franklin Fountain.

Antiques adorn the space. 1920s music tinkles. Original tin foil ceilings look down upon the circular tiles of mosaics in faded green, burgundy, and yellow. Black blades of old-fashioned fans slowly spin, and attached red ribbons flutter. Outside, a fading sign proclaims "Ice Cream Sodas." Like a quilt, three yellow and mahogany squares sit on top of a large framed in dark red, reading "warm desserts", "hot chocolate", and "coffee."

The neighborhood is known rightfully as Old City. A few blocks away from Franklin Fountain, a house-sized frame traces the original structure of Benjamin Franklin's final home and print shop. He, the first "American" and inventor, is the namesake of Franklin Fountain. In the field guide for soda jerks, it reads: "We celebrate Franklin's humor, his creativity, his homespun philosophy, and his democratic approach to making all people happier."

Philadelphia locals brighten when Franklin Fountain enters the conversation. "I don't know why I never knew about it!" they say. "It must have been around forever!"

As I recount this comment to Eric Berley, a co-founder of Franklin Fountain, he gives a knowing smile underneath a trimmed mustache. This is success to him. The word "timeless" is dropped throughout our conversation. Franklin Fountain embodies the Historic Mile as if it has always been in Philadelphia since the city's beginning. Unlike Franklin Fountain's candy store, a rebirth of the Shane Confectionary established in 1911, Franklin Fountain was an idea to reinvent ice cream parlors, to reflect the nostalgia, and to re-create "simple times" to bring people together.

That type of nostalgia reflects the Berley family history. Eric and his brother Ryan grew up in an antique-filled house. After Ryan was born in the 1970s, their mother, Carole, began selling antiques from their home. Their living room was laid out like an old-fashioned ice cream parlor. The family was surrounded by history much like Philadelphia, a city of pivotal historical moments.

In 2002, the Berley family purchased a building in the Old City neighborhood. Feeling stagnant in their current career paths, the brothers brainstormed ideas for what to do. Through a family connection, Eric traveled to New York to hone his skills in making ice cream under the tutelage of an expert ice cream chef. Working with his brother Ryan, they concocted a business plan, bringing together their love of antiques and old-fashioned ice cream parlors. They wanted a place with the warmth of the modern Starbucks, but filled with memories. Eric describes the pre-World War II era where Norman Rockwell's illustrations graced the covers of the Saturday Evening Post and weekends involved an ice cream dish at a neighborhood shop. He

summarizes the rationale, "Small America."

An ice cream parlor was the answer. History and nostalgia were bundled in one place. At the time, a bakery called Eroticakes, selling provocatively shaped baked goods, inhabited the space of today's Franklin Fountain. But the brothers dug through the space's history, discovering a former convenience store and a German American Bar, Schmidt's. On the ground, the Berley discovered oyster shell fragments, reminders of former visitors. Franklin Fountain opened to the public in the summer of 2004.

This beginning was not the end of their vision. Around the corner, the Berley brothers renovated and reopened a candy shop, Shane Confectionary, located in the same building. Antique display cases are full of candy. Above Franklin Fountain and Shane Confectionery, the Berley brothers plan for a museum to educate the public on the old-fashioned confection process. A copper machine sits several floors above, ready to churn sweets. Waffle irons are open to make cones. Like a library catalog, small green drawers hold original candy molds. There are cannons, shells, and merry-go-around horses. They are antiques, by today's standards. A note hangs at the base of the machine reads in script, "Please Excuse our Appearance as we Restore this Machine." Cooling racks hold freshly made chocolate. In a narrow hallway below the candy factory, ice cream reigns. A refrigerator is filled with plastic-covered canisters with handwritten labels. One states today's date: "5-13 peanut butter."

Today, Eric leads the ice cream development, and his brother Ryan oversees the confections. The brothers developed a menu reflecting the nostalgia of "a forgotten past." Consisting of malts, milkshakes, and classic ice cream, the menu contains nuanced flavors, enhanced by a modern touch. Phosphates, a drink once thought to be medicinal, is a fizzy beverage mixed with citrus and raw egg. In ice cream, vanilla heightens peach. Baked goods are housemade. The Berley brothers played with flavors using ginger, orange, and lemon. Does mint work with coconut? How about Cuban mint? Is there way to make an ice cream with coconut milk and no dairy? A mango liquor and Indian mangos adds layers to the mango sorbet. "These combos twist the product," Eric says, smiling. "We are not a fly-by-night quality of ice cream."

In the best way possible. Organic is a keyword. The Berley brothers want fair trade ingredients. They demand quality taste. Eric describes tasting different bananas, a range of pistachios, and raisins.

The line of customers spills into the street. Older ladies with red hats chatter about flavor decisions. Once inside, they study framed menus, black text on white, which describe fountain drinks and ice cream specialties. A small sign on the white-painted tin wall says, "Terms: Cash, Legal tender may be obtained, SW Corner, 2nd & Market Sts." Customers check their wallets for bills.

A narrow wooden frame holds wooden slides, each embossed with an ice cream flavor: standards like vanilla and unique nostalgics like teaberry, a throwback to the popular Clark's teaberry gum in the 1960s. Modern technology hides beneath a 1910 cash register.

Behind the counter, soda jerks, dressed in Victorian white uniforms, take the orders and tell customers to move to the end of the counter. The soda jerks follow the mantra: "Eat to please thyself, but dress to please others." Women wear an apron, black skirt and a snood—a Victorian hat that drapes across the hair. Men wear a cap and apron.

A customer fills a paper cone with water from a ceramic dispenser. A lamp with an ornate black shade glows. Glass jars of waffles, confections, and delicate flowers fill a shelf. Ice cream to go is packaged up in Chinese take-out boxes. On a mirrored cabinet of colored syrups, a bust of Benjamin Franklin, topped with a black hat, peers at the visitors as they arrive.

Outside Franklin Fountain, the line of customers grow. A man and his son devour a banana split towering with whipped cream and balls of ice cream. The soda jerk, wearing a striped hat, nods. Three scoops of ice cream rest in a glistening silver metal bowl. A glass bowl of hot fudge is pushed toward me. "This is the best way to have ice cream," Eric says, and I drizzle the hot liquid over teaberry, vanilla, and chocolate ice cream.

Underneath a gray jacket, he wears a dark-colored button shirt and a striped bowtie in shades of blue. He wears vertical striped pants fastened with suspenders. He is young, and he thinks of the future of nostalgia. Customers, replete with the ice cream, put their empty dishes into a metal tub.

A Franklin Fountain manual from 2011 proclaims their values to a budding soda jerk:

> The Franklin Fountain aims
>
> To serve an experience steeped in ideals,
>
> Drizzled with drollery,
>
> And sprinkled with the forgotten flavors of
>
> The American past.

When I walk out of Franklin Fountain, I feel Philadelphia's Old City and all its history beaming beneath my feet.

Bassetts Ice Cream

Bassetts Ice Cream has experienced over a century of American history at its Reading Terminal location through seven generations of the Bassett Family. Founded in 1861, Bassetts continues to serve classic ice cream flavors like butterscotch vanilla and rum raisin.

bassettsicecream.com

45 N 12th St

Philadelphia, PA 19107

(215) 925-4315

Near the side doors of the Reading Terminal Market lies Bassetts, an ice cream counter lined with stools. Scoopers dig up ice cream, and their waiting customers watch the action unfold. Located next to stalls hawking cheese and sandwiches, Bassetts has seen history over the past 150 years of its existence—the train service roaring above the public market until 1984, the decreasing business in the 1980s after the train terminal moved, and the rebirth of public markets in 2000.

Indeed, the Reading Terminal is described in *Philadelphia in 1868*, a guidebook for members of the American Pharmaceutical Association:

...here the thrifty yeomen of Delaware,

Chester, and Montgomery counties may be

Seen selling mutton, veal, beef, and poultry

Of their own raising and preparing, 'pound butter,' the product of their won dairies, with

All the vegetables and fruits in season fresh

From their won gardens and orchards.

From Philadelphia in 1868

(Lippincott's Press, 1868)

The Reading Terminal Market is the city's revered treasure today, and just as described in 1868. The plans for the new train terminal including razing of the public market. Merchants protested, "You're taking away our space!"

The city relented and built the train terminal above the market, a compromise guaranteeing a flow of customers from departing and arriving trains.

Today, plaques on the wall celebrate the building's long history. A display case showcases small pyramids of chocolate squares. Another case displays fresh catches of lobster, fish filet, and crab. Gyros are prepared behind another counter, and the smell of fresh-grilled meat fill the air. The famous sandwich stand is sold out. "Man vs. Food! Bizarre foods!" a boy whispers. A bakery shows its wares—layered cakes as small as the palm of a hand, and cookies in a rainbow of colors. A customers leans in at the sausage stand and asks, "Do you have any more of that spicy one?" A young man moves his knife across roast beef, creating feathery slices. "Next!" a woman shouts from the cheese stand.

At Bassetts, the ice cream counter extends the entire length of the stall. Swinging onto a stool, Michael Strange tells me the story— the history of the Reading Terminal, the founding of the ice cream company, and his reluctant journey to become CEO. Michael motions at the stalls around us. "You tell me if you run into an ice cream shop that spans more than six generations. We are the oldest ice cream shop in the country."

Indeed in 1861, Michael's great-great grandfather Lewis Dubois Bassett began making ice cream in Salem, New Jersey using a mule-driven machine. Soon, he began selling ice cream on Market Street and Fifth Street in Philadelphia. Lewis was a Quaker school teacher and farmer. When a space opened up in the Reading Terminal Market in 1892, Bassetts moved into the market.

What customers don't know is that Bassetts is the one merchant that remains from the original Reading Market Terminal. By the 70s, train service had moved underground, away from the public market. The flow of customers slowed to a trickle, and merchants began leaving. At one point, Bassetts was one of the twenty stalls remaining in the cavernous space. Even with empty space, they continued to serve ice cream.

In the midst of the decline, Ann Bassett, the president of Bassetts at the time, prepared to close the business. But young Bassett family members protested—this was a place of memories. "Let me continue it!" Michael insisted when he discovered his mother's plan, and pushed sandwiches into the Bassetts product line.

"After all, Bassetts put a lot of us through college," Michael recalls.

Indeed, Michael started working at Bassetts in the sixth grade. Bassetts served ice cream the classic way—on a dish—and his primary role was to clear the empty dishes from the counter. He remembers rumbling trains that shook the dust from the ceiling. By the tenth grade, Michael scooped ice cream for customers. In college in the seventies, he continued scooping to earn money. At the time, he never planned for a career at his family's ice cream business. With the pending closure of Bassetts in the 80s, Michael transitioned to leading the Bassett family business after college.

Today, Michael boasts about the expanding international business. Bassetts reached China in 2008. After testing green tea varieties, he designed Bassetts' green tea ice cream, to amplify the taste of matcha. Inspired by the traditional moon cakes served during the Chinese Mid-Autumn Moon Festival, he created moon cakes with ice cream. "James Sun," Michael drops the name of his Chinese business partner. "He's so well-connected."

Michael jumps to logistics and cost, thoughts are spinning in his head. During transit over the Pacific, the container is maintained at -20°F for an optimal storage temperature for the ice cream. "But guess what?" he says and widens his eyes. "It's cheaper to send ice cream by train to Chicago than it is to send ice cream to areas around Philadelphia by truck. The energy to maintain the temperature for either is such a difference."

Michael developed many flavors, beyond the Bassetts' original eight flavors. Chocolate marshmallow never became a good seller. Undeterred, he developed vanilla butterscotch. He experimented with key lime pie with pie chunks for an ice cream competition. Michael came up with the idea of ice cream molds. "We need to change with the times and will always keep updating," he says.

Yet the stand maintains its original structure, frozen in time. The marble counters are the same as 121 years ago. Until the recent international expansion, ice cream was made fresh on premises in the basement of the Reading Terminal building. A black strip runs along the awning of Bassetts with the words "ice cream", "L.D. Bassett Est. 1861", and "Cheese." Above, paintings depict the Bassett family—there is Michael's mother and himself in a blue apron. A Bassett sign hangs in the shape of an ice cream cone. Customers stand and study flavors on a sign. I walk up, making quick decisions. A scooper wears a blue shirt and smiles. I gravitate to the raspberry truffle and the English toffee (conjuring Heath crunch).

Tourists pour into the Reading Terminal market from a tour bus. The building, like other destinations in Philadelphia, is a historical landmark. "Ice cream is a fun product," Michael says.

Woodside Farm Creamery

Woodside Farm Creamery converted their family dairy into an ice cream business. Using dairy from the farm, classical ice cream flavors like black raspberry chip and butter brickle are served during the warm months.

woodsidefarmcreamery.com

1310 Little Baltimore Rd

Hockessin, DE 19707

(302) 239-9847

I am dropped into the bucolic nature of Delaware. The rolling hills here remind me that this isn't a place of skyscrapers and concrete. Pulling off a freeway, I find Woodside Creamery nestled in beside barns and houses. Made from eight planks of wood, a sign declares in hand-painted green with white outlines: "Woodside Farm" and "Farm Fresh". "The Creamery" and "Homemade Ice Cream" are painted in white.

"This used to be rural," Janet Mitchell, the co-owner of Woodside Creamery, explains. "Now it's really suburban."

Her husband, Jim Mitchell, is the seventh generation in his family to own the farm in Hockessin, a community in Delaware. The Mitchell family started the farm in 1796 when George Washington was president. Years ago, the suburban sprawl was contained within the metropolis—45 miles to Philadelphia and 10 miles to Wilmington. Back then, the green pasture expanded over the rolling hills. Paying homage to the Native American Lenape tribe that once lived in Delaware and the land's scenic beauty, Hockessin stems from the Lanape word "hokesa," meaning "pieces of bark." Once a community known for dairy farms and mushrooms, Hockessin today is an affluent residential community that surrounds the busy Lancaster Pike, a quick shot to Wilmington in Delaware and Newark, New Jersey.

Yet even now, with broad thoroughfares paralleling the farm, Woodside Creamery retains its original intentions. It is a family farm at its heart. In the mid-nineties, the farm started a herd of cattle—thirty Jersey cows—with the goal of selling directly to the market. Instead of focusing on profit, they wanted to maintain a traditional dairy farm. Cheese was sold and transported to Washington D.C. Within the last decade, they've decided to make changes to keep with the times and appeal to the growing population in Hockessin. "We wanted to make Woodside more than a farm," Janet says.

The Mitchells went to take the short course in ice cream making at Pennsylvania State University. In the spring of 1998, Jim and Janet opened the ice cream shop, Woodside Creamery, to answer the increasing population in the area. Initially, the shop was a porch with two dipping cabinets. Outside, a simple hay wagon with plywood advertised the creamery with hand-painted words "Homemade Ice Cream." Jim and Janet spent the first two years after opening getting the ice cream shop in order. They focused on using quality ingredients—Grade A milk from their cows when possible and using local produce for the flavors. Soon the news of an ice cream shop spread through word of mouth. The dairy was prized for its quality, harking to the words "farm fresh."

"This is a community-embraced destination," Janet says. "We know a lot of people in this area. My husband's family has roots here. The community has embraced this place."

Like the exterior hand-painted sign, flavors are hand-painted on white horizontal slabs. Playful drawings circle each flavor. The letters of "Rocky Road" appear to be shaky. Sketches of fruit accompany "Banana" and "Strawberry." White letters are outlined in black for "Coconut." A sign hangs from the ceiling that reads "Custom dipped to your appetite," followed by handwritten prices and alternates to a scoop like milkshakes and banana splits. Scoopers dig up ice cream from rectangular boxes, chosen so that they don't spin.

Over thirty teenagers move in and out through Woodside Creamery learning to scoop as their first job. Janet teaches them to interact with the crowd. They must work together to make an extraordinary ice cream experience and cover the hardest night, Fridays. "I want to hear 'you have friendly and smiling kids'," Janet says. "I have had kids five to six seasons and watched them go to college."

In a small building next to the shop where families flock in during the weekday afternoon, Janet sits in an office decorated much like a living room. Jim oversees the wholesale side of Woodside Creamery while Janet manages the books and retail of Woodside Creamery. She is a part-time veterinarian for small animals and has been practicing for more than twelve years. "I live what I do," Janet says.

Outside, I watch Jim clean out the barn. He wears a green and brown jacket. Cows amble through the pastures. In a smaller building, flavors churn through production in a sterile room with silver humming machines and large plastic tubs. Certain custom-made ice cream flavors made here, Janet tells me, that are not sold at Woodside Creamery, but sold elsewhere. Janet brags about the ghost pepper ice cream, derived from a pepper known as the world's hottest chili pepper, sold at The Ice Cream Store in Rehoboth Beach.

In the production room, two young men in baseball caps buzz around, organizing and filling containers with freshly churned ice cream. One takes a pitcher of chocolate ice cream and pours it into a packing funnel. Another places the lids on the quarts of ice cream. A freezer room holds labeled cardboard boxes of ice cream. The smell of ice cream custard envelops me. "Over the years, there's trial and error to find the right flavors," Janet says. "Like how much coconut in a flavor. How much vanilla to add."

On a wooden bench, we sit next to the door to the ice cream shop. I dip into a dark-colored ice cream with green-tinted caramel swirls named "Motor Oil," concocted to resemble 40-weight oil. The combination of coffee and caramel creates layers of nuttiness and sweetneess. I am not a fan of gimmicks, but I love the way this flavor is sold to car-related events like NASCAR and car shows. "Steam Oil Motor Oil" was the original name, Janet tells me. Despite the flavor's inedible appearance, its popularity soared.

The sun moves toward the horizon. Jim moves hay bales and jumps onto a John Deere tractor. Janet talks about how her father-in-law still milks the cows, and how she hopes that her environmentally-savvy niece will take over the business one day. She wears a black jacket with a pinned ribbon and blue jeans. Her hair is shoulder length and she sighs thoughtfully. She points at the original ice cream machine, nestled in a display cabinet next to a plaque detailing the history of the farm. She and her husband live over the hill, on the same land as Woodside Creamery.

Traffic builds in the distance, and the light glints over the shiny cars. The cows rest in the green pasture. The sun oozes orange over the rolling hills. Janet watches as a car swings into the parking lot, kicking up dust. A family spills out, and a little girl sprints for the door of Woodside Creamery. A couple walks to the surrounding lawn with an ice cream bowl in hand.

"I miss it during the wintertime," she says, referring to her time off between Thanksgiving and March. "This is a basic simple family farm."

Spiced Apple Ice Cream with Caramel Swirl

Peel, core, and dice apples.

In a saucepan, combine diced apples, honey, vanilla, cinnamon, allspice, nutmeg, and lemon zest. Mix well and cook over medium heat, stirring often until apples are tender, and little liquid remains.

If the spiced apples are solid, mash with a potato ricer or puree in a food processor. Set spiced apple mixture aside to chill in refrigerator.

Preheat the oven to 425 degrees. Pour the entire can of condensed milk into a glass pie plate or similar baking dish. Stir in salt. Cover the pie plate with aluminum foil. Set within a larger baking dish, like a large cake pan. Add hot water to the larger baking dish until it reaches approximately halfway up the side of the pie plate.

Bake for 60 to 90 minutes. Check the water level every 15 minutes. Add more hot water to maintain the water level halfway up the side of the pie plate. Carefully remove the pie plate when caramelized and browned. Once cool, whisk until smooth.

Refrigerate dulce de leche if not used immediately. When chilled and ready to use, warm up in the microwave or in a warm water bath.

Combine cornstarch and 2 ½ tablespoons of the half and half in a small bowl. Mix, until there are no lumps, to create a cornstarch slurry.

In a separate large bowl, whisk cream cheese and a pinch of salt until smooth.

Whisk the remaining half and half, sugar, and corn syrup in a saucepan set over medium heat. When the mixture begins to steam, add the cornstarch slurry. Continue to stir until the mixture thickens, about 1 minute. Gradually whisk the hot milk mixture into the cream cheese mixture until smooth.

Pour the spiced apple mixture into the base. Mix to incorporate ingredients together.

Chill the mixture at least three hours or overnight in a refrigerator.

Scrape cold mixture into a pre-frozen ice-cream-maker bowl and churn according to manufacturer's instructions.

Scoop the spiced apple ice cream into an empty container. After every scoop, swirl in a generous spoonful of dulce de leche. Freeze up to a month. To serve, let stand at room temperature until slightly softened, about 10 minutes. Serve as is, or with slices of fresh apples.

7

Vancouver

"Every city in the United States is exactly like every other city in the United States, with maybe New York and San Francisco the only exceptions. Vancouver seems to be defying globalization."

- Douglas Coupland, *City of Glass*

In downtown Vancouver along tree-lined streets, more than five languages float. There is English, spoken with a hint of a British accent. There is also Cantonese, French, and Arabic. Restaurants are international—from steaming bowls of ramen to donër stands hawking meat from a spinning rotisserie to food truck salads of chickpeas and puffed rice. A couple raves, "It tastes like street food in India, but better."

Vancouver changes. I have visited it three times, each separated by a decade. When I was ten, I remember the endless Chinese food and expansive houses of my parents' friends, who left Hong Kong before its reunification with China. Ten years later, when I was twenty, I returned to Vancouver, a stopover before Alaska. I discovered malls with Hello Kitty shops and a large park adorned with flowers. When I returned another ten years later, I saw new piano shops, omnipresent green bins, ample bike lanes, and an efficient subway system, results of the Winter Olympics. This city stands in for the backdrop of movies and TV shows. It represented San Francisco in the 2014 remake of Godzilla and the American Northwest in the Twilight movie series.

"The mountains can guide you," a friend advised me, as I began my journey in the city. "They are always to the north."

Vancouver locals love their food. As for dessert, gelato is the undisputed favorite ice cream in Vancouver. Vancouver and Seattle are similar despite being located in two countries. They share a similar climate, a similar culture, and similar beliefs. Yet, unlike Seattle, Vancouver did not develop a booming ice cream culture. The ice cream scene in Vancouver has room to grow.

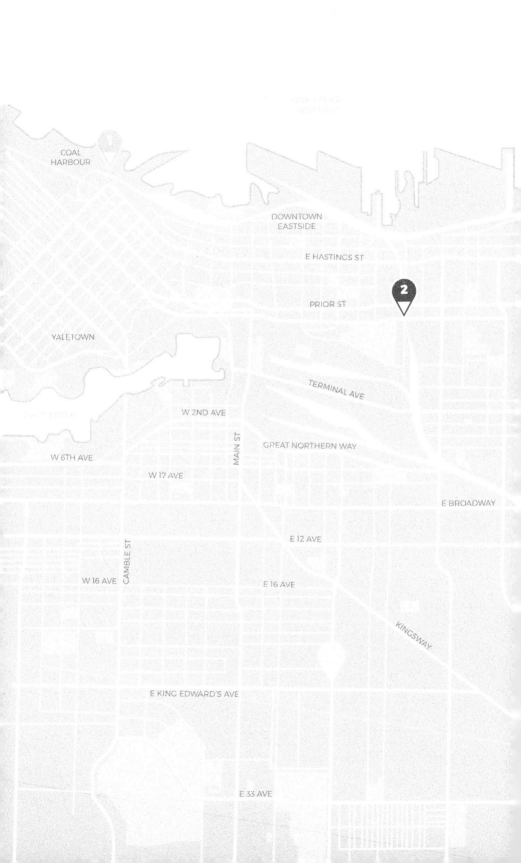

Bella Gelateria

bellagelateria.com

1001 W Cordova St

(604) 569-1010

Earnest Ice Cream

earnesticecream.com

3992 Fraser St

(604) 428-0697

La Casa Gelato

lacasagelato.com

1033 Venables St

(604) 251-3211

Bella Gelateria

Bella Gelateria makes gelato with passion, winning gelato contests across the world. Trained at the world-renowned Gelato University and admired across the world, the owner maintains traditional, old-fashion gelato methods.

bellagelateria.com

1001 W Cordova St

(604) 569-1010

"Passion over product," James Coleridge repeats through our conversation. "It's all about passion over product."

Passersbys view Bella Gelateria's kitchen from a window on the busy West Cordova Street, located near the waterfront in downtown Vancouver. Office workers on their lunch breaks and children out of school roam into the small shop. A black and white checkerboard floor reflects European design. James greets familiar faces as they enter the elegantly decorated shop and flow into a line near the display cases. A board lists the flavors. Customers are encouraged to choose the number of scoops and then choose the flavors.

Two large vertical machines continually spin behind a glass divider. They pump up and down, mixing a secret recipe. If one peeks through the glass divider, the color may hint at the churning flavor. Chocolate? Hazelnut? The finished gelato is stored in glittering metal canisters that are tightly covered with matching lids.

James wears black-framed glasses and studies the small kitchen. As he discusses his craft, he gestures wildly and repeats the word "passion." Glistening buckets of ingredients fill the cramped space. Fresh gelato is primarily crafted here in this kitchen. Salvatore, his assistant from Italy, moves swiftly through the kitchen, carrying pots and bins. He speaks little English and converses with James in Italian. "We met at Gelato University," Salvatore says. "When James invited me to Canada, I said, 'Yes, absolutely'."

The stove heats a large stockpot of milk, which will caramelize into dulce de leche or thickened sweetened milk. This version of dulce de leche is not a home cook's quick version—James does not steam a can of condensed milk for sixty minutes. "We take fourteen hours to make ours." James says. "We make it from scratch."

Nine months later, I meet instructors at the Gelato University in

Italy. I mention the story of James, a gelato maker from Vancouver. They chuckle at their memory of him. One says, "He's crazy. I have never met anyone so passionate."

Retiring from a twenty-two year career in politics, James searched for a new purpose and inspired by his first taste of high-quality gelato in 2003, he turned to the art of gelato craft. After studying at the Italian Culinary Institute and Carpigiani's Gelato University, he opened Bella Gelateria in 2010 on West Cordova Street.

Accolades arrived quickly to Bella Gelateria. With the same energy dedicated to his career in politics, he aims to maintain the authenticity of his gelato by using whole, raw ingredients and producing gelato with traditional methods. Even in a city burgeoning with gelato shops, no other shop is as dedicated to using such high quality ingredients. Other shops prefer using imported syrups and powders. James is different. He has deservedly earned the label "crazy."

In 2011, James was the first non-Italian to win the international award called, "Gelato Pioneers—Father," given by Carpigiani, the gelato company behind Gelato University. The award highlighted his success in spreading the craft of artisan gelato across the world. The following year, Bella Gelateria earned first place at the Gelato Festival in Florence, Italy, for both the "Technical Jury" and the "People's Choice" awards.

James is dedicated to his craft. Out of the first twenty ice cream shops that I contacted, he responded first, within eight minutes of my initial email to him. When we meet, he darts between scooping gelato and chatting with customers.

He begins our conversation with an important question: "Do you know the difference between gelato and ice cream?"

James launches into the world's gelato situation. Many ice cream lovers have forgotten or never had high quality gelato. In fact, they, as he observes, have only tasted industrial-made ice cream. James laments that consumers do not know the true taste of mint. Rather, they describe mint ice cream as bright green with a faint hint of an artificial mint flavor. James' mint gelato reflects mint as a core ingredient. The idea of seasonal ingredients are lost on consumers.

"There's less fat and sugar in gelato," James says. "That's because we use a lot of whole foods to make our flavors." James describes the method for crafting the base for gelato. This base is the first step for production of ice cream or gelato. His voice transitions into a professor-like tone, lecturing about water constituting 87% of milk, and the natural added sugar coming from fruit like strawberries. He criticizes other ice cream artisans for neglecting traditional steps to make gelato and ice cream. "If the base is the same for a nut flavor and a fruit flavor, then that's wrong," he says. "Something is not right."

Bella Gelateria is not a low-cost, rapid operation. Strawberries have been carefully selected for gelato. Vanilla beans, rather than vanilla extract, are used; although the beans require additional time to extract their flavor. Unlike most gelato shops, each gelato flavor is stored in an individual temperature-controlled metal container. James tracks his progress with an extensive recipe book, which he uses to calculate the differences between flavors, and he balances the amount of fat and sugar to craft the perfect gelato.

"The flavors match the weather profile," James says as he looks outside.

It is August. The summer sun breaks through the morning clouds, warming the streets. "Fruits are great right now," James says.

The world's diversity inspires the flavors at Bella Gelateria. Flavors like akbar mashti, tiramisu, crème brûlée, and yuzu citrus reflect a diverse palate. Having grown up in multiple countries in North America and Europe, James maintains a global perspective of the world. In his travels, he came across foods that embodied the ingredient. Food need not be complex. After all, a simple vanilla flavor is perfect by itself.

Local friends from Vancouver walk me to Bella Gelateria after we finish a spectacular Asian meal. With cups of gelato in hand, we make our way to the waterfront and watch the last ferry depart for North Vancouver. "I love to send my coworker down to Bella Gelateria to get a quart of gelato," a friend says. "It's our post-lunchtime treat."

"Everything is a choice in gelato," James says. "It's about quality over quantity. Passion over product. This is my quest to be perfect. I want to protect the guardians of gelato."

La Casa Gelato

La Casa Gelato, located in a pink building in the neighborhood of Strathcona, boasts over 500 flavors including durian, double espresso, and garlic. Originally from Italy, the owner achieved his lifelong dream of making gelato and continually experiments with new flavors.

lacasagelato.com

1033 Venables St

(604) 251-3211

"I want customers to walk in and say, 'Wow!'" Vince Misceo, the owner of La Casa Gelato, repeats. Dressed in a short-sleeved button down shirt, Vince looks around the shop with pride. His bushy mustache hints at his Italian heritage.

In the midst of all the concrete buildings in Vancouver, La Casa Gelato rises as a pink oasis adorned with Canadian and Italian flags. Pink was deliberately selected to calm customers and contrast the industrial neighborhood. It represents Vince's lifelong dream of opening a gelato shop.

As we stand near the registers, Vince lifts his head up to greet every customer who visits. Of course, the regulars. Even the tourists. The tourists stand out in the crowd—they tiptoe into the shop, raising their eyes to the 218 gelato flavors. The shop is spacious, allowing for ample room for customers to move from display case to display case. The scoopers ask overwhelmed customers easy questions to help them make their decisions: "What do you like? Chocolate? Strawberries? Do you want something refreshing, or some rich, milky goodness?"

The scooper pauses and suggests a flavor to match the person's preference. The customers buy the scoops and head outside.

Across the street from La Casa Gelato, an illustrated mural of old-world Italy surrounds a small garden adorned with wooden benches and beds of colorful flowers. In the morning, at the stroke of 11 AM, the outside lights snap on, and the shop opens for gelato. Scoopers wearing black and red aprons or black La Casa Gelato t-shirts prepare the shop for the day's business. One employee crosses the street to clean out the debris from yesterday evening—a happy moment of gelato now remnants of used spoons and empty La Casa Gelato cups.

Born and raised in Italy, Vince cherished the summers where lemon gelato was served during festivals, celebrations, and neighborhood gatherings. Lemon, his favorite traditional flavor, reminds him of his childhood in the old country. Vince corrects my false assumption, that gelato finishes each Italian dinner. On the contrary, gelato was a special treat for his family or a summer celebration. "Not everyone could afford to have gelato," he says.

When he was a teenager, his family moved to Vancouver to look for better opportunities. Vince began his career picking strawberries and digging for at local farms. Later, he moved to work in construction and factories, Yet Vince recalls, "It just wasn't my cup of tea."

Vince had a single dream: to open a gelato shop. Starting with twelve flavors (one was lemon, of course), he opened a shop that sold its product primarily to restaurants. His gelato served as a "refresher" between rich and heavy courses in Vancouver restaurants. After several years, he discovered that his competitors made cheaper, larger productions of gelato. His business struggled. Adjusting his focus, he directed his energy to creating surprising flavors. Every day, he asks the most important question: what new flavor can I make today?

Highlighted in travel guides to local newspapers, visitors from Singapore to India to the United States started to patronize La Casa Gelato. Greetings in every language, and multi-colored country flags in reds, yellows, stripes, and stars decorate the walls. "That's my country!" visitors point out when they enter.

Encountering diverse cultures in Vancouver, Vince wanted to satisfy their preferences with flavors like durian (a well-loved Asian fruit that tastes like sweet cheese, but smells like rotting flesh), and akbar mashty (a Persian delight of saffron, rosewater, and pistachio). He boasts, "I want seventy percent of people to say, 'This flavor is better than in my home country. It tastes like I'm actually eating the fruit.'"

All flavors are crafted from whole ingredients, without any extracts or syrups. Over five hundred individual flavors are made throughout the year. Sourcing high quality ingredients, Vince invests time for produce like traveling to farms to pick up fifteen pounds of wild asparagus or growing wild herbs like fennel in the garden behind La Casa Gelato. Although he lacks familiarity with all fruits and spices, Vince spends time researching, tasting, and experimenting. "This is the magic," he smiles.

Occasionally, a customer disagrees that the flavor does not match the fruit. They protest, "This isn't cherimoya! This isn't mango." Vince shakes his head, as if looking at an invisible customer. He says, "You say it is not, but only one of us is right."

Yet some flavors elude him. Marmite (a savory spread popular in the United Kingdom), kimchee (spicy pickled cabbage from Korea), and salmon with chocolate are some examples. "Yet, I love it when people say, 'What the hell is this?' and they like it!" Vince says and gestures at the display cases. "What you see here is what you get."

Asian customers crowd the shops during the peak hours, causing their favorite flavors—durian, lychee, and mango—to empty out of the bins. For his lactose intolerant customers, Vince makes sure that ten percent of the gelato is dairy-free. His adventurous customers ask for the daring flavors like wild porcini mushroom, hot banana, spicy mango, and pear gorgonzola with blue cheese.

"I was the first person in Vancouver to import passion fruit - the first!" he describes his proudest achievement.

Because Vancouver's weather and city architecture match that of American cities, Hollywood routinely use the Canadian locale as a backdrop. As a result, many celebrities drop by La Casa Gelato. Photos and autographs from Martha Stewart, Richard Branson, and pop culture icons adorn the walls. "Movie stars deserve to be treated like regular people," Vince says. "I want them to be left alone."

His five-year old granddaughter watches the customers. During summer vacation, she comes to the shop daily, ready to scoop gelato. Whether the customer wants hot banana or strawberry, she nods, her eyes lighting up with instant recognition. Despite the over 218 bins of gelato, she jogs without hesitation to the desired flavor's location behind the display case. Pulling a stepstool, she climbs up with a scoop and opens the display case. Dipping deep into the bin, she presses gelato into a La Casa Gelato cup. When a writer from CNN came to interview Vince, he brought his younger daughter, who played with Vince's granddaughter. During the few hours he spent at the shop, the writer remarked, "My daughter has learned a lot more about ice cream here than she will in a decade of eating it."

"I just want to make this shop better," Vince says. "My wife knows that at night I am always dreaming up a new flavor."

Earnest Ice Cream

Earnest Ice Cream makes ice cream in small batches with flavors like whiskey hazelnut and lemon poppy seed. Adhering to their value of a small environmental footprint, Earnest Ice Cream stores ice cream in reusable glass jars and delivers by tricycle.

earnesticecream.com

3992 Fraser St

(604) 428-0697

Green-conscious. Artisanal. These two adjectives drive the core beliefs of Earnest Ice Cream.

Outside of Woodland Smokehouse, a cooperative kitchen in the Grandview-Woodlands neighborhood, the Earnest Ice Cream tricycle rests between trips to sell and deliver ice cream at the local markets. Its large cooler lugs up to six flavors of ice cream—from whiskey hazelnut to mulled pear. Inside the kitchen, industrial freezers store labeled jars of fresh ice cream. Residing among donut bakers and barbeque chefs, the founders of Earnest Ice Cream, Ben Ernst and Erica Bernardi, extract the flavors from hazelnuts and whiskey for a small batch of ice cream. The ice cream base, once completed, churns in an ice cream machine, an Emery-Thompson that can make twenty-four quarts a day. Then, jars are filled with the fresh ice cream and carried to the freezer to harden.

Despite late-night ice cream ice cream, in the morning Ben and Erica bound from their kitchen to the retail storefront of Woodland Smokehouse. Erica says, "We were making whiskey hazelnut ice cream last night. We had some because we were hungry."

They chatter like childhood friends. Ben wears a white t-shirt and perches his tall frame on a stool. Erica oversees marketing, and she stops to chat. Dressed in blue, she exudes bubbly friendliness. They laugh when I ask them to describe what flavors they think they are. Exchanging trusting glances, Erica says, "Tart raspberry, of course. I am fiery and savvy."

Ben says, "Maple walnut, because I am methodical and investigative."

"I am a pretty avid cyclist," Ben says. "Also, we want to show people how we run our business. We want to set the example that it is possible to have a low carbon footprint."

Ben's love of ice cream stretches into his childhood. Growing up in the United States, Ben's parents took him and his brother on frequent road trips. Bored by passing the same landscapes, they would chant, "Dairy Queen! Dairy Queen!" When they would pull into a Dairy Queen parking lot, the two young brothers would rush inside to grab a frozen treat. Not by coincidence, Ben worked at a Dairy Queen later at his first job. After he moved to Bellingham, Washington for college, he frequented Ballard's, which was the popular ice cream shop in town. Unsurprisingly, he got a job at Ballard's learned even about making ice cream. He settled in Seattle after college, where his passion for ice cream grew as new ice cream shops began to open in 2008. Having worked at a company that made messenger bags from recycled materials, he wanted to make a sustainable impact on the local community.

But then he moved to Vancouver. "I met a woman and married her," Ben explains the relocation to his wife's hometown. "My friends know me as the guy who loves ice cream."

In Vancouver, Ben wanted to do something different. He observed that although Seattle's culture was similar to that of Vancouver, the city lacked good artisanal ice cream. In Vancouver, he had become friends with Erica, his wife's roommate. As Ben and Erica chatted, they discovered their shared love of ice cream and decided to open an ice cream business together. Neither Ben nor Erica had prior experience

with running a business. To better understand ice cream, they both went on individual journeys to develop their own philosophies for Earnest Ice Cream.

On her own, Erica traveled through Europe, from London to Lisbon, where she tasted all kinds of ice cream. Using her previous restaurant experience, Erica studied the subtleties and specialties of the various ice creams. In the Netherlands, the ice cream was as soft as whipped cream. In Italy, local ingredients enhanced the flavors of the gelatos.

Ben cycled around the United States with his wife during their honeymoon, stopping by local restaurants and stands. Burgers and donuts popped out of deep fryers. But the ice cream stands caught his eye. Their fresh, soft serve ice cream tasted unlike anything he had ever eaten. He learned was that great customer service could make or break any business, especially the ice cream business. Crafting a great product is not enough. "You have to own what you're doing, like using high quality ingredients instead of easier-to-find, cheaper choices," Ben says.

The flavors at Earnest Ice Cream are carefully crafted to integrate the products of local businesses with customers' childhood memories, like dessert from a distant past. Erica says, "We have a farmer who sells us raspberries, and he had a special request for raspberry cheesecake."

Working with local regions to represent Canadian flavors, Ben and Erica developed a whiskey hazelnut ice cream flavor. They developed oatmeal crisp with cooked rhubarb, emulating was a childhood dessert. They play with new flavors three times a week. These experiments are sent to a small group of tasters for approval.

Like the oatmeal crisp, salted caramel, the signature flavor of Earnest Ice Cream, harks back to childhood memories. "It reminds me of a candy that I used to eat," Ben says. "Some customers have said that the salted caramel flavor has changed their lives." When they realized that many ice cream shops already had a version of salted caramel ice cream, Ben and Erica concocted a less intense version of salted caramel. The process is simple. They caramelize the sugar until it is dark and then mix it with cream. The addition of the cream immediately halts the process. Salt and butter add to the flavor's richness.

"This is good ice cream," Ben says, as he sticks a spoon into a sample jar. "The density, the amount served, the mouth feel, and the texture."

From enhancing flavors with sour cherries to candying marshmallows, Ben and Erica learned useful techniques from purveyors at the farmers markets and the fellow craftsmen who worked at Woodland Smokehouse. When they were working on developing an ice cream sandwich, Ben and Erica tested multiple cake recipes to produce a strawberry dacquoise cake that dissolves at the same rate as the ice cream melts. That way, the doughy texture would not remain with each bite. Earnest Ice Cream uses whole ingredients and milk from Avalon Dairy, a local dairy. The real fruit and foods that anyone can buy in a local grocery store add to the intensity of the product's homemade, rustic feeling.

"Sometimes mistakes happen." Erica says. "There was one time that ice cream spilled on the floor, causing us to lose an expensive batch. It was all over the floor and the door!" Ben sighs, remembering the lost batch of ice cream.

Suddenly Olive, Ben's wife, races through the front door of Woodland Smokehouse. Her eyes shine through her glasses. She pauses her run to ask, "Where's the ice cream?" Ben smiles and gestures toward the kitchen, "You can probably find a few pints in the freezer." As Olive jogs to the back of the shop, I ask about the inventory, which is one of Ben's responsibilities. Ben says, "We're working that out. We are casual."

Roasted Peach Sorbet

5 to 6 peaches   1 cup sugar

1 tablespoon brown sugar   Pinch of cayenne (optional)

Juice of 1 lemon   Pinch of salt (optional)

Halve the peaches and remove the pits. Sprinkle the brown sugar over the peaches. Roast for 30 minutes at 400 degrees until soft. Remove from the oven and let rest for a few minutes.

Peel the skin from the peaches. Be careful, as the free-flowing juice and peach flesh can be very hot. Roasting brings out the flavor and should make the skin easier to peel. If the skin is not easy to peel, leave it on, which adds texture to the sorbet. Strain the skin out before churning if the texture is not desired.

Mix juice of 1 lemon and sugar in a blender or food processor. Add the roasted peach mixture and puree until evenly mixed.

Optionally add a pinch of cayenne and a pinch salt to intensify the flavors.

For best results, chill the mixture for a few hours, although the mixture can be churned immediately if at room temperature or cooler. Scrape mixture into a pre-frozen ice-cream-maker bowl and churn according to manufacturer's instructions.

The sorbet is best served immediately. To store, scoop roasted peach sorbet into an empty resealable container. Freeze up to a month. To serve, let stand at room temperature until slightly softened, about 10 minutes.

8

Taipei and Around

The most common greeting in Taiwan is not "hello," but "have you eaten yet?"

In a land where sharing food is a sign of love, desserts are no exception. It's my kind of nightlife—the never-ending rows of food booths offering steaming noodle soups, freshly made papaya milk, and salt-and-peppered fried chicken. Despite being Chinese American, Taiwan was a country that was foreign to me. Born and raised in California, I was more familiar with Hong Kong, the former colonial island city where my parents originated.

Taiwan, on the other hand, is an independent nation born out of the Chinese Civil War in the 1950s, with a multi-party democracy and a prosperous economy. As one of the four Asian Tigers, Taiwan is known for their information technology manufacturers like HTC. Most importantly, the Taiwanese love food in a way that I had never encountered. "Come," they say. "Try the roasted duck, the braised cabbage, and these handmade dumplings of pork and chives."

Secrecy is part of their nature. "I can't let you see anything," a Chungli City ice cream shop owner tells me, protecting his multi-generation recipes. I press him, but he smiles, not rising once in our conversation. Instead, he says, "Have the red bean ice cream. It's delicious."

In this part of Asia, the philosophy of feng shui permeates everyday behavior. Feng shui goes far beyond interior design—it is the balance vital to maintaining good health and life. In this part of the world, "hot" tends to refer to foods that increase blood flow like fried foods. "Cold" refers to cooling foods like watermelon. Temperature is irrelevant. Doctors several centuries ago perceived cold foods as evil, with the idea that cooling the body leads to disease. Locals still believe that eating ice cream or shaved ice treats the body poorly. A local friend even shook his head at me and reminded me to be careful.

Dairy is a new phenomenon, growing in recent decades. Young people fill up trendy cafes, indulging in cold desserts. Near the Sun Yat-sen Memorial, a popular ice cream chain Big Tom invites locals to experience "real" American ice cream or *bing chee ling*. A blind saxophone player plays to the locals sitting outside eating large sundaes. With an entrenched history with Japan, this is the second-best place to experience Japanese culture. At a hip café, they gobble down American breakfasts of stacked waffles and pancakes. Then they indulge in bowls that were more like dazzling bouquets of cranberries on toothpicks and melon cut into assorted shapes. I order a special ice cream sundae. On the menu next to its photo, words shouted "magic!" and "disappears!" I tip a small mug of espresso over the bowl. Instantly, the cotton candy melts into a syrupy mess, revealing the hidden scoops of vanilla ice cream. Ice cream, regardless of its origin, is a status symbol—a fancy scoop, in a land of foodies, signifies good taste. The fervor impresses me. Many prefer the grand scale of decoration, yet I sought a shop that practiced small batch, artisanal ice cream. I found one shop, and it contained the beauty of ice cream.

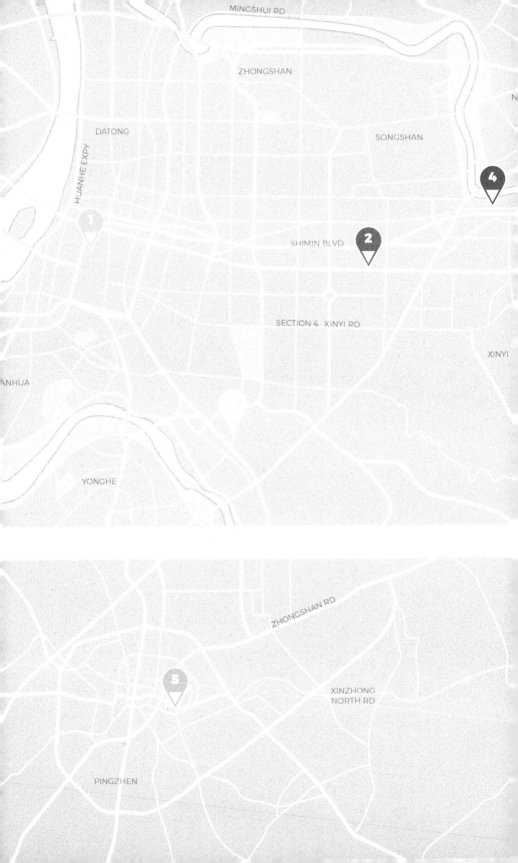

Snow King (雪王) ⭐

snowking.com.tw

No. 65號2樓 Wuchang St

Section 1
Zhongzheng District,
Taipei City
+886 2 2331 8415

Ice Monster

ice-monster.com

No. 297號 Zhongxiao E Rd

Section 4
Da'an District
Taipei City
+886 2 8771 3263

Tai Yi Milk King

No. 82號 Xinsheng S Rd

Section 3
Da'an District
Taipei City
+886 2 2363 4341

Ice Cream Burrito at Raohe Night Market

Guangzhou Street and Xichang Street

Raohe Night Market
Songshan District
Taipei City

Yi-Sin Fruit and Ice Shop

No. 15 Heping St

Zhongli District
Taoyuan City
+886 3 425 9697

Snow King (雪王)

Snow King (Xue Wang) spans three family generations. Over seventy-three flavors such as guava and tofu are served at this small shop that is frozen in time, located a few blocks from the bustling Ximending, the "Times Square" of Taipei.

snowking.com.tw

No. 65號2樓 Wuchang St

Section 1

Zhongzheng District,

Taipei City

+886 2 2331 8415

Kao Ching Feng shifts on his perch, and words spill out.

"*Bing chee ling*!" he says, teaching me the word for ice cream in Mandarin.

I speak Cantonese, a dialect of Chinese common in Hong Kong where my parents grew up, unlike the melodic Mandarin spoken in this large island of Taiwan. The ice cream is scooped behind a counter and placed in my hands in glass bowls. If not for a grandfather's fervor and his grandson giving up a profitable job, Snow King wouldn't be here today.

On a nondescript street a few blocks from the bustling Ximending shopping district, a white garage door with red and white Chinese characters rolls up, sending a clang down the short street. Xue Wang, literally translated to English as Snow King, is open for business. Unlike nearby shops, Snow King lacks corporate influence. Over seventy-three flavors such as dragon fruit and tofu are served at this small shop that is frozen in time, just blocks from the famous Ximending, the "Times Square" of Taipei.

Unlike nearby establishments, white tiled walls dominate the space. Three handwritten signs demand a smoke-free environment. Steel tables shine with the reflection of the fluorescent lighting, surrounded by small wooden stools like those in a classroom. In the kitchen, a fan blows. The freezer hums. Conversations echo through the small shop. Pedestrians rush by, forgetting this old shop, located on a side street away from the busy few blocks of Ximending. A scooter roars by. A park across the street is unoccupied.

For the first hour of opening, the shop is empty. Then customers start trickling in, scanning the menu. In the back, someone thumps and carves ice, the sound reverberating through the small space. Ice cream churns in the back daily to ensure freshness. Seeds from mangoes and lychees are pulled from the fruit flesh.

Arriving initially on a Sunday, a friend and I scan the menu in Chinese, barely recognizing words that we learned at Chinese school as children. Noticing our struggle, a woman hands us a menu in Japanese. Japanese tourists are common in Taipei. We smile shyly and I shake my head. My friend asks in American-accented Mandarin, "Do you have a menu in English?" Realizing that we must be Chinese American, she hands us a different menu. English translations are handwritten and carefully taped to the menu. Samples are not offered here, and we jump headfirst into ordering. We try the fresh flavors—basil, watermelon, and guava. The scoops are served in glass bowls. Much like the fruit, I roll the guava on my tongue, sensing the grittiness and tart sweetness. The basil bursts with a fresh herbal scent with each spoonful. The scoop of watermelon ice cream is filled with seeds. An American urban myth says that watermelon will grow in your

stomach if you eat the seeds, but that fear does not exist in Taiwan where watermelon seeds are commonly roasted and served as snacks.

A few days later, I return with a fluent speaker of English and Mandarin. Kao, the third generation owner of the shop, is energetic as he laughs about the history of Snow King. Wang or king in English is a common word to add to any Asian establishment much like the words "lucky" and "gold". The hope is that literal descriptions help the shop. He describes how as a child, he used to play in and around the freezer, watching his grandfather make ice cream. He remembers his daughter at the age of 6 months trying the taro, dark chocolate, and guava. He explains in halting English and then fluent Mandarin about the seventy-three flavors. "Because my grandfather believed that he could make one more flavor than the 72 changing shapes of the Monkey King," he says.

I chuckle. As a child, my mother told me stories of the Monkey King, an epic fable of a mischievous, rebellious monkey who acquired godlike powers, flying at high speeds on clouds and somersaults. His best trick: the shape-shifting power of 72 transformations, which gave him power to shrink to the size of a feather or grow large into a lumbering giant.

Kao smiles as he perches on a table. He leaps to the counter when a customer enters, ready to showcase the flavors. He is a third generation owner of the shop, born into the business in 1979. Along with his sister, Kao operates the shop today. Their grandfather opened the shop in its current location in 1947, dissatisfied with the previous shop and a mobile cart. The first flavors for the business were taro and kidney, unique flavors to Taiwan, made in a hand-cranked machine.

After their grandfather passed away, the shop stopped making new flavors but did progress to ice cream machines. Kao refuses to create new flavors, intending to maintain the same recipes. New flavors were created regularly when his grandfather was alive—flavors like pork floss (a popular Chinese snack, like beef jerky with cotton candy texture), or the popular Japanese azuki beans. Customers are awestruck by the flavors—sesame oil chicken, beet, and pig knuckle—and discover that the ice cream tastes as described. "It's very special!" Kao says. "When I was young, I tried everything. I was the family taster, but my grandfather was the master taste tester."

Snow King regulars order red bean and watermelon. The Japanese visitors get lychee and peach, Kao notes, and Hong Kong visitors order curry and wasabi. Kao enjoys watching two female visitors try curry chili, their faces prickling in surprise with the taste. Kao lists his highlights—the cheap but high quality bananas, the carefully selected blueberries, the juice used for the starfruit ice cream, the jasmine honey obtained from an organic farm in eastern Taiwan. A custom recipe exists for each flavor to enhance its intensity.

"People eat ice cream everyday like noodles," Kao says. "I want the nostalgia of the fifties. Food is mixture of sweet and salty."

Visitors come from Japan, Hong Kong, mainland China, and Malaysia. Guidebooks and social media draw young people to the shop. Couples introduce their children to the shop, a popular destination for many Taiwanese adults. Overseas Taiwanese from the United States visit Snow King. They want to touch their roots. "When people see the flavors, they are not just for them, but also for older generations," Kao says.

But the industry is not safe. Kao winces as he thinks about the future—whether Snow King will still be present in a decade. Foreign ice cream businesses, such as Häagen Dazs and Coldstone, have penetrated the Taiwanese market. "I am scared some people will like that too much," Kao says. "But then some don't. I will stay with what everyone enjoys. I don't combine flavors into something like mint chocolate chip."

"This street is famous," Kao says and looks to the empty park. "There used to be a movie theater. This is a family place. It has never changed. Everything is the same. I will not sacrifice quality even though it requires a lot of physical effort."

The neighborhood's face has changed since the early years. Foot traffic has shifted east, where teenagers rush to dazzling displays of ice cream, fruit, and cotton candy. Kao describes a former butchery in the neighborhood. He frowns as he remembers the owner's son taking over the butchery. "When he had a chance to make money, he decided to close the shop," Kao says. "Nobody wants to do a blue collar job. I have to support my family by working remotely at an insurance company. You see, the art in ice cream is maintaining the art."

Pur-Erh Ice Cream

Stir milk and heavy cream in a medium saucepan over medium heat, until mixture starts to steam and bubbles start to form at sides of pan. Remove from heat. Add the tea leaves, and steep the tea in the mixture for at least an hour. Strain out the tea leaves. Strain once more if any major leaves remain, but feel free to leave a few bits to give the ice cream visual hints of the flavor.

Pour into the same saucepan. Stir the steeped mixture with ½ cup sugar over medium heat, until mixture starts to steam and bubbles start to form at sides of pan. Remove from heat.

Whisk egg yolks and remaining sugar in a large bowl. Wrap a damp kitchen towel around the base of the bowl (to prevent it from slipping). Gradually whisk in half of hot cream mixture. Return entire mixture to saucepan set over medium-low heat. Stir with wooden spoon constantly, until mixture is thick enough to coat the back of the spoon. Pour through a fine sieve into a metal bowl. Let stand for 10 min. Then lay plastic wrap directly on surface to prevent skin from forming.

Chill for at least three hours or overnight in the refrigerator. Scrape cold mixture into a pre-frozen ice-cream-maker bowl and churn according to manufacturer's instructions.

Scoop ice cream into an empty resealable container. Freeze up to a month. To serve, let stand at room temperature until slightly softened, about 10 minutes.

Shaved Ice in Asia

Like the fabled origin of ice cream, snow with fruit and sweet toppings reigns in Asia. Its location near the equator means humid weather—perfect for farms growing fresh fruit like ripe mangoes and coconuts.

Nearly every Asian country has a version of shaved ice. In the Philippines, each region has their own variation of halo halo—meaning "mix mix" in Tagalog. This is shaved ice layered with colorful tapioca, flan, *nata de coco* or coconut jelly, and ice cream. In Korea, *patbingsu* is a creamy ice cream topping layers of shaved ice and fresh-cut fruit. In Taiwan, the shaved ice cream is mixed with sweetened kidney beans and taro bits, drizzled generously with condensed milk. In Hawaii, heavily influenced by Asia, snow cones are flavored with syrups. Some ice is so finely shaven that when mixed with evaporated milk, a spoonful tastes like ice cream without the feeling of melted water. When local names are translated into English, sometimes they are given as snow ice or snowflake ice.

Yet unlike ice cream shops, components of shaved ice cream are made outside of the shop. Gelatin may come pre-packaged from grocery stores. The ice cream is made by big brands. Snow ice creators boast of the combinations—their craft lies in the cobbling of ingredients.

While roaming through the endless malls in Manila, I come across popular Filipino cafes, serving variations of halo halo. At Chowking, a facsimile of a Filipino McDonalds, the halo halo is served in a thick, red, plastic cup. The beats of David Guetta back up the voice of Sia as she croons "Titanium" overhead. The ice of the halo halo freezes into a solid piece before I can dip a spoon to gather a taste of the dessert. At the Peninsula hotel in Makati City, servers clad in suits deliver decorated bowls of an endless variety of mix-ins—sweet garbanzos, *pinipig* or pound young glutinous rice, *ube* or purple yam, *macapuno* or Filipino coconut, jackfruit strips, red, green, and white *nata de coco*—all topped with ube ice cream and leche flan. At Razon's—an eatery found in malls—unlike its other Filipino counterparts, the halo halo is nearly all white without the colorful tapioca. Halo halo there is simple, focusing on the quality milk. Servers balance four glasses of the beige mixture on trays as they serve it at tables. In one spoonful, the sour taste of tamarind bursts on my tongue. At a nearby table, a child squeals in delight while playing on an iPad. On a small island in the untouched tropical Palawan, a bowl of halo halo looks like a syrupy mess of white and purple. Yet a spoonful of this halo halo revealed its creamy balance of all ingredients. No one ingredient dominates another. Evaporated milk blends the flavors for a creation that changes with each spoonful. Outside Manila in non-commercial areas, the presentation of halo halo is less important.

In Taipei, a friend and I find a famed hot pot shop that provides

"ice cream" as the cooling dessert. During the traditional dinner, pots situated in the middle of each table are filled with hot broth where diners dip raw meats and vegetables to create an unique self-serve meal. My friend asks for the special dessert. Instead of pushing the button to heat the pot, the server pushes a hidden button. A fan below the table roars to life, cooling the pot to freezing temperatures. Soon, the server places bowls of red, green, and yellow liquid on the table. With a swift motion, the female server pours a single bowl into the pot. The syrup drips across the surface, slowly filling the circular space. As she scrapes it with small metal paddles, the syrup forms small crystals. Moments later, a snowflake consistency forms over the surface. The server expertly scoops the "ice cream" into our plates. I taste a small spoonful of the light green "ice cream".

"I taste green," I say.

"Yes, that's what I think it is too," my friend says and laughs.

With hesitation, we finish the rest of the bowls, rolling the colors on our tongue. The red bowl tastes like red. The yellow bowl tastes like yellow. It's not cherry, banana, or green apple. I taste the colors, reminiscent of artificially flavored candies.

My boyfriend's family friend gets word that I am on a quest to find ice cream. She brings my boyfriend and me to Big Tom, the newest name in ice cream in Taipei. "I think that Big Tom came from Seattle," she says. "Very famous!"

I notice that the English slogans are awkwardly written throughout the shop. In fact, the business was conceived as a chain of ice cream shops that recalled the American way of living. A collection of ice cream scoops is displayed along the wall. Taipei 101, the tallest building in the country, rises above a small manmade lake and glitters with lights. A blind musician sits on a wicker chair in the outside garden and plays a saxophone. His music echoes with the tones of the fifties and sixties. The faces of those dipping into the ice cream are older and upper class.

A local friend hurries me to the real Taiwanese food gems—the night markets that stretch for more than ten blocks, filled with vendors hawking fried dumplings and noodle soups. In the center of the Raohe night market, he shows me a cart with a large center stone. A woman takes a thin crepe. In the middle, she piles layers of chopped cilantro,

crushed peanut brittle, and three flavors of ice cream—taro, pineapple, peanut. It crunches as I take each bite. She calls it an "ice cream burrito".

Finally, I discover classic Taiwanese shaved ice. At classic institutions like 216 Tapioca King and Tai Yi Milk King, a bowl of taro, mango, glutinous rice balls, sweetened kidney beans, boiled peanuts, almond jelly, and a sweet jelly fungus is the crucial dish, ordered frequently by the elders. The delicate sweetness oozes out and melds with its surrounding layers. Young people opt for the fresh fruits—the passion fruit, strawberries, and kiwi. I watch a special request for mango pudding as it swirls round and round the shaved ice. "This is what I remember from childhood," a local says. "Ice cools the body."

9

Manila

Upon arrival at Ninoy Aquino International Airport, the primary airport in the Philippines, the flurry of activity is an instant culture shock. In metro Manila, locals wander through mazes of malls. Traffic, a bane for many Manila residents, is unpredictable, and a slow commute is guaranteed. Sprawling neighborhoods dominate metro Manila. The historical Intramuros, the original city center, lies to the northwest while the financial institutions and middle-class areas of Fort Bonifacio and Makati lie to the southeast.

Food blogs and mobile apps like Foodspotting dominate the food culture. Every Filipino I meet argues over the best *chicarrones* (fried pork rinds) and *halo halo*—a shaved ice dessert, with the fervor of an American football fan. Locals are natural foodies.

Educated Filipinos speak fluent American English. Many of their relatives live in the San Francisco Bay Area. Inspired by San Francisco ice cream shops, artisanal ice cream businesses are homegrown. Their culture insists on family values, and young Filipinos are expected to work for their family businesses. Ice cream, to them, is a hobby, supported by ample staff.

The world of Manila will always be two sides of a dream to me. One undesirable side: the nightmarish parts of never-ending traffic and the humidity, the loud uncomfortable roar of air conditioners. The other treasured side: the beautiful things like untouched islands and the passion of the locals.

It's the latter that reflects my time in the Philippines—like two films I viewed before arrival. One was a zombie comedy about homosexuality repression. Another depicted a family in Mindanao, the war-torn island. Both spoke of hope for change. This reflected in the locals. Like the taxi drivers who stayed calm. Like the American expat who plans to stay indefinitely and crafts ice cream at his Fort Bonifacio sushi restaurant. "There's so much more room to grow here," he says.

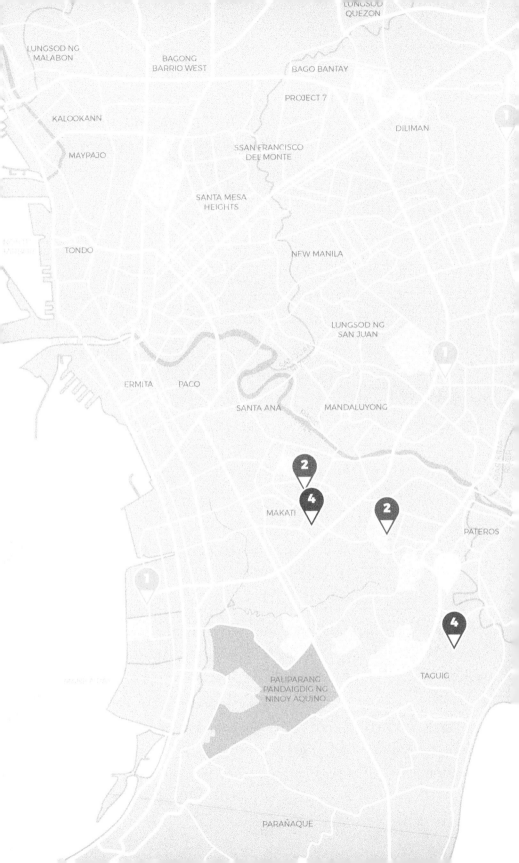

Sebastian's Ice Cream
facebook.com/Sebastians.Ice.Cream

The Podium

> 4th floor, near escalator
> 12, ADB Ave
> Doña Julia Vargas Avenue
> Ortigas Center
> Mandaluyong
> +63 927 453 7426

SM Mall of Asia

> New Entertainment Mall, 2nd Floor (near IMAX exit)
> Seaside Blvd
> Pasay City
> +63 915 489 5753

Regis Center

> Ground floor Lobby
> Katipunan Ave (in front of Ateneo)
> 327 Park 9
> Quezon City
> +63 927 290 1633

Carmen's Best
carmensbest.com

The Market

> 156 L.P. Leviste St
> Salcedo Village
> Makati City
> +63 2 887 2993

Tower 1 Icon Residences

> 26th St. Cor. 3rd Ave
> BGC Fort, Taguig
> +63 2 519 3025
> +63 932 875 3292
> +63 939 284 3444

Adam's Seriously Good Ice Cream
facebook.com/AdamsIceCream

The Grand Hamptons Tower

> Bonifacio Global City
> 31st Street
> Taguig City
> +63 917 898 2826

Merry Moo
merrymooicecream.com

Salcedo Saturday Market

> Salcedo Park
> Salcedo Village
> Makati City

Mercato Centrale

> Corner of 25th Ave and 7th St, in front of The Forum
> Bonifacio Global City
> Taguig

Sebastian's Ice Cream

Sebastian's Ice Cream experiments with local and foreign tastes. From a green mango sorbet with shrimp paste to fried ice cream wontons, the ice cream flavors continually change and push boundaries.

facebook.com/Sebastians.Ice.Cream

The Podium

4th floor, near escalator

12, ADB Ave

Doña Julia Vargas Avenue

Ortigas Center

Mandaluyong

+63 927 453 7426

SM Mall of Asia

New Entertainment Mall, 2nd Floor (near IMAX exit)

Seaside Blvd

Pasay City

+63 915 489 5753

Regis Center

Ground floor Lobby

Katipunan Ave (in front of Ateneo)

327 Park 9

Quezon City

+63 927 290 1633

Think different are the words that come to mind as I sit and listen to Ian Carandang, the owner of Sebastian's Cool Comfort. Unlike many Filipinos I have encountered since landing four hours ago, his English is impeccable and his stature resembles a teddy bear. He drapes over his seat outside, blending in with the other visitors to his shop. Charisma emanates from his eyes as his steady voice describes how Ben & Jerry's changed him, especially through their cookbook. He goes on about the visits to duty free shops that inspired him, by allowing him to taste Ben & Jerry's and Häagen-Dazs and understand how the quality of ingredients affects the depth of flavor.

Behind the counter, he shows me his latest creation. In a boiling bath of oil, he drops ice cream encased in won ton wrappers. A minute passes, and Ian drops them onto a plate. "Not many people have seen this!" he says about the process.

Ian is proud. I request a visit to his kitchen in Quezon City. In his reply, he says, "My kitchen there isn't really presentable. My shop in Mall of Asia will give a better look at the stuff I do."

This is where we are today. The Mall of Asia sprawls over multiple football fields and is the 10 th largest mall in the world. Store after store demands attention—from the blaring electronics to sparkly clothing. Maps are of no use, containing disconnected numbers and shop names. I spin around an indoor theme park, electronics shops, and clothing shops until I discover an outdoor walkway. Tucked in a corner and appearing like a fishbowl, the ceiling to floor glass walls of Sebastian's Cool Comfort invites mall goers competing with frozen yogurt and other cold desserts. It is nearly December here, but the tropical location of the Philippines creates a humid environment.

The cool air from the air conditioner blows over me as I enter. Three Filipino women serve and gossip in Tagalog, the local conversational language. They hushed as I approach the glass display case. Flavors are categorized as traditional or premium. Vanilla, chocolate, and mint chip sit in tubs, maintained at a scooping temperature. I scoot over to the premium section, determined to taste the more exotic. A woman hands me a sample of the blueberry cheesecake cookie dough, a layered mix of the ingredients. Now the Filipino flavors. The sapin sapin flavor, described as "the most popular flavor" by the woman behind the counter, slides down my throat—a mixture of taro and

mango, a reminder of the traditional Filipino dessert. The *latik* or reduced coconut milk adds a slight crunch. I spot a flavor inspired by a traditional Filipino appetizer, green mango slices with *bagoong*, fermented shrimp paste. The green mango sorbet reminds me of the lightly spiced green mango in Vietnamese salads. The *bagoong* layers the green mango sorbet in a black, thick paste. Its taste is so intense to my Americanized palate that I am uncertain whether to feel disgusted or elated. Near the entrance, a large group of female customers chatters in Tagalog and fawns over a newborn baby. Plush ice cream cones hang on the wall-a plain one, one adorned in neon yellow pink, another doused with chocolate, and a simple yellow. Once I order a scoop, a scooper immediately appears at my table with a glass of water. She then returns behind the counter.

For his entire life, Ian like many Filipinos experienced the typical Pinoy flavors—ube (purple yam), queso (cheese), and chocolate. Low-end mass ice cream manufacturers are common —like Magnolia, an ice cream brand found in supermarkets throughout Manila and even the United States. *Sorbetes* also prevail in that space. Häagen-Dazs dominantes the high-end ice cream. Little exists between Magnolia and Häagen-Dazs. "There is no innovation in *sorbetes*," Ian laments. "At Ben & Jerry's, I had Cool Britannica. Then there was Wavy Gravy and Chunky Monkey."

He smiles as he thinks back on his first taste of ice cream in 2005. "My metabolism was faster then," he observes. "I got my aunt to order ice cream from Amazon."

Ian had managed a BBQ restaurant. In the kitchen, he made ice cream to serve ice cream. Yet, the ice cream did not attract immediate customers. By chance, Lori Baltazar, a local food blogger at *Dessert Comes First*, discovered the ice cream. She wrote about it, and business boomed.

Classmates who studied business pitched in to help with logistics and operations. Ian studied cookbooks—from Matt Lewis and Renato Poliafito's *Baked: New Frontiers in Baking* to David Chang's *The Momofuku Cookbook*, testing recipes on his own. Ian planned to make a wholesale business, selling to restaurants. But soon, he realized Sebastian's Ice Cream embodied a special brand. He opened three shops in multiple malls. But as his business started, frozen yogurt became popular. The recession dragged down business, and he struggled. Eventually, his family helped him out. Eventually, his business climbed back while several frozen yogurt shops closed. "I am grateful for the dark ages," Ian says. "We went through a lot of hell."

The downturn helped him figure out what worked. He felt stubborn, unwilling to give up on his passion. An episode of *Top Chef* inspired him to make cheesecake with Concord grapes. In figuring out a flavor with cheesecake, he tasted the standard dessert and thought about how to deliver the same flavor. Use small chunks, he remembers. While developing a flavor with cake, he observes, "Cookies are better than cake. Cake crumbles."

Filipinos have been slow to catch on the local, organic movement moving across the world. A food culture in the Philippines dictates preference for food from abroad. Many visitors are surprised that Sebastian's Cool Comfort is local and uses local ingredients, whenever possible. Beyond dairy, milk, and cream, all other ingredients come from sources near Manila. "I want to do it right," he says.

Opening a location near a school, local students piled into his shop. Their palates welcomed experimentation to satisfy their curiosity. Ian dreams of expansion, especially to other cities in the Phillipines. Cebu and Boracay are his next steps. But his goal is to build the next comforting flavor, which he says, will always bring the next visitor.

Carmen's Best

Carmen's Best, created by the grandson of a beloved president of the Philippines, uses dairy from the family's farm for its rich ice cream. With no storefront, Carmen's Best provides take-home ice cream with simple flavors of butter pecan and Spanish almond.

carmensbest.com

The Market

156 L.P. Leviste St

Salcedo Village

Makati City

+63 2 887 2993

Tower 1 Icon Residences

26th St. Cor. 3rd Ave

BGC Fort, Taguig

+63 2 519 3025

+63 932 875 3292

+63 939 284 3444

Paco Magsaysay, the owner and founder of Carmen's Best, meets me in the grand high-ceiling lobby of the Makati City Peninsula Hotel, today decorated with angels and white lights. It is November, and the city is preparing for the holidays. Upon spotting me, he strides across the lobby filled with palm trees and ornate couches. A tinkling piano plays somewhere above us.

The historic hotel opened its doors in 1976 to impress international delegates arriving in Manila for a global conference. In the following years, the hotel became a symbol of economic prosperity for the Philippines in the developing country.

The choice of meeting location is apt. As we sit, others pass by and acknowledge Paco with a nod. Unlike the businessmen roaming around the lobby, Paco wears a blue checkered short-sleeved button shirt and slacks. He carries a quiet demeanor. Once he starts talking about ice cream, he becomes more animated.

We order the Peninsula Hotel halo halo, a dessert that consists of layers of shaved ice, local Filipino fruits, tapioca, crunchy rice, and ice cream. Recognized in 2006 as the "best legal high" according to *Time Magazine*, the halo halo whisks away the heat with each milky spoonful. As we dive our spoons into the layers, Paco observes that the *ube* or purple yam ice cream isn't at all like his.

Paco is no stranger to this world. As the grandson of a popular and beloved Filipino president Ramón del Fierro Magsaysay and the son of a senator, Paco endures the attention that comes from his family legacy. During his grandfather's term, the administration was corruption-free, and the country flourished internationally in economic growth, sports, and foreign affairs.

"Don't steal," Paco recalls his grandfather's words. "I want a 100% clean name."

Like many Filipinos, Paco spent some time in the United States. In the early eighties as a twelve year old, he moved to the United States. Every Saturday, when he lived in San Francisco, he took the bus to Pier 39 to play video games. When he ran out of money for video games, he then went to Ghirardelli Square for his treat. He laughs as he tells the story, "My two scoops of vanilla ice cream with butterscotch and extra nuts was my weekly reward to myself!"

Looking back, he never thought the weekly treat would have such a big influence on his life. Returning to the Philippines in 1993, he entered the family business. The ice cream was never supposed to happen. His family owned a dairy farm complete with the cows, pasteurizers, and homogenizer to produce cream. The family could not sell all the product, though. "Dairy farms are hard," Paco says.

On return visits to the United States and ice cream shops like Bi-Rite Creamery in San Francisco, he realized that nobody made ice cream from scratch in the Philippines. Inspired, he decided doing that would help get rid of the family dairy's excess product.

With a priority on quality, he aimed high. At first, he attempted to make fresh gelato, but the cost was exorbitant. Inspired by the *Ben & Jerry's Homemade Ice Cream & Dessert Book*, he jumped into creating ice cream, using their sweet cream base recipe. Knowing his audience in the Philippines preferred sweet flavors, rum raisin and other savory flavors were never part of his plan. He experimented with variations in the dairy fat to give ice cream the best flavor and variations in the overrun, the air in the ice cream, to achieve the right texture and mouth feel. He delivered small orders of pints, and the reception was tremendous.

"I didn't realize that it was going to be that good," his customers say upon the first taste.

Given this success, Paco started Carmen's Best Ice Cream in 2009. He named the shop after his daughter Carmen because he believed that the business deserved a feminine name.

In Manila, when people think of ice cream, they think of Paco. Tied closely to Carmen's Best Dairy, the ice cream production allows Paco to control of every step in the process. "A to Z," he describes the ice cream. "I am the only one in Manila who has a dairy farm."

The ice cream, available only in pre-packaged tubs, is produced in the outskirts of Manila, about a ninety-minute drive from the center of the city. Every day, part-time cooks craft the ice cream. Then, because of customers reluctant to drive for the dessert, ice cream is delivered through to the metropolitan region.

The price point of the ice cream does not scare Paco. "People want to pay for quality," he adds.

Customers marvel at the exoticism and love the plain flavors—the butter pecan, the vanilla. Locals want the exotic flavors and gravitate toward anything American. "But in America, everything is too sweet," Paco says. "I changed it."

After experiencing the halo halo, Paco pulls three tubs from a freezer bag. Each tub is emblazoned with "Carmen's Best"—white text on blue—on the top and the sides. The words "pure indulgence" in elegant white script sits below the name. Still covered in frost, I make out the handwritten words in uppercase letters of each flavor—butter pecan, salted caramel, vanilla, and turrón—a special flavor based a traditional Spanish Christmas candy of almond nougat.

"This is the cream of the crop," he says.

The ice cream has naturally gotten to the right scooping temperature. The cream of the butter pecan slides down my throat and leaves a lingering satisfying finish. I lick my lips. The salted caramel ice cream is buttery, the savory taste rolls up to the roof of my mouth and disappears into the sweet caramel. In the following days, I snack on the ice cream for breakfast and for dessert after dinner.

He loves watching the facial expression of customers as they first taste the ice cream. Paco observes my surprise disappearing into pleasure when I taste salted caramel. But ice cream is not his entire life. He jokes about being a single father in his forties—"Nobody wants that," he laments. "I have other people sell for me. I focus on experimenting." But perfecting ice cream is his "side job". Despite the success, he still works in the technical industry. As I talk to other food entrepreneurs in Manila, this pattern repeatedly emerges. With family legacy and expectations, food is not a career for the educated elite.

"Integrity," Paco repeats at the end of our conversation. It was a summary of everything we discussed—his desire to remain true to the craft and adding attention to detail. "I believe in quality."

Merry Moo

Merry Moo was born out of inspiration from traveling and a desire to bring unique quality ice cream to Manila. Existing as a side project, Merry Moo draws locals to its stand at markets and a newly opened shop.

merrymooicecream.com

Salcedo Saturday Market

Salcedo Park

Salcedo Village

Makati City

Mercato Centrale

Corner of 25th Ave and 7th St, in front of The Forum

Bonifacio Global City

Taguig

"Maybe I can tour you around a weekend market in Salcedo on Saturday morning?" Kelvin Ngo, the founder of Merry Moo, says during our flurry of emails across the Pacific Ocean. "And then, we'll have ice cream!"

Before meeting Kelvin, local bloggers and I visit Mercato Centrale, a night market of prepared foods. Sellers hawk the fried pork and rice bowls, letting its savory smells beckon passing customers. In a corner of the market, ice cream lovers crowd around Merry Moo. Several feet behind the booth, a portable generator quietly rumbles, maintaining the scoopable temperature for the ice cream display case. Unlike many stands, the Merry Moo staff lean forward, offering samples following Kelvin's instructions, "Spot people who are shy and offer them a free sample."

In the strawberry basil ice cream, the basil's herbal flavor highlights the vibrant flavor of the strawberries. As I taste the Earl Grey, a hint of lemon wraps around the tea. Continuing our stroll through the market, we each carry a white cup with a smiling cow and the brilliant green lettering of "Merry Moo."

A more kind and generous host than Kelvin would be hard to find. Merry Moo hosts an ice cream stand at the weekend market. But Kelvin insists on meeting at a Starbucks in Makati City. Arriving at the café, a shy smile ripples across his face, bursting with optimism. He beckons, and I follow him to a parking garage.

We drive through the snarling traffic to the residential high-rises. During the humid November morning, Kelvin wears a bright yellow polo shirt and gray shorts. Tapping on the gas pedal with white boat shoes, we inch our way in a sedan.

Despite the excitement in his emails, Kelvin possesses a quiet demeanor in person. His eyes light up at the mention of international food and culture. Unlike the cuisine of neighboring countries, Filipino food, according to Kelvin, lacks presentation and simplicity. A visit to Vietnam cemented the idea that simple, quality food with modest presentation is possible. Focusing on real ingredients, Kelvin wants to educate his customers that great food is possible without impact to the environment. "Just as the Filipino cuisine is a melting pot of different cultures from our history, so is our ice cream, which is a mix of different flavors from around the world." Kelvin says.

As he describes the ice cream shop in Singapore—the primary inspiration for Merry Moo, his eyes widen. "I am a frustrated chef and foodie," he says. "Manila needed ice cream like that."

Choosing Philadelphia-style ice cream without eggs, Kelvin perfected his signature flavor of sea salt caramel through cycles of experimentation—iterating on variations of caramel. Like many native Filipinos, he grew up eating *sorbetes*. Surprised by creamier ice cream

abroad, he believed that Manila deserved a delicious cold treat.

Typical of many Filipino households, the kitchen help supported his ice cream flavor experimentation. Following shows like *Iron Chef*, *MasterChef*, and Mario Batali's *Molto Mario* he aimed to infuse food with his creativity. Initially, Kelvin made ice cream for friends and family, who repeatedly suggested, "Why don't you sell?"

In 2010, Kelvin came across an ice cream-making contest from a popular Filipino blogger, Anton Diaz of *Our Awesome Planet*. The "Ultimate Taste Test" invited local food bloggers to sample food purveyors from French macarons to *longanisa*, Filipino-style sausage. The response was tremendous. Tasters devoured Kelvin's ice cream with frenzy, rating it the best of the show. Now with confidence, he started at Mercato Centrale, and the buzz spread by word of mouth. Found at outdoor food markets, perfect for the constant hot weather of the Philippines, his ice cream beckons a passerby with classical flavors of sea salt caramel and Earl Grey to experimental flavors like Pop Rocks & mallows and Chinese salted egg.

"But Merry Moo is just a hobby," Kelvin says. "I work full-time selling watches for the family business."

As we arrive outside the Salcedo Community Market, the bustle of the market reaches its mid-morning peak. Expats started Salcedo Community Market in 2004 to bring people together through local and organic homemade food, inspired by European-style outdoor food markets. Inside the market, rows of prepared foods and produce glimmer in a rainbow of colors. From freshly fried *chicharrones*, pork skins, to fresh cashews from southern provinces to Thai-style *halo halo*, the food enthralls any empty stomach. Proud to show off his country and heritage, Kelvin leads me through the market. His quiet demeanor disappears when he spots unique food. "Try this!" he says, placing a sample of sticky rice in my hands.

He fills my arms with sweet, sour, and salty foods. Mango sticky rice wrapped with banana leaves. Quiche from a French expat. Local crickets. Pig intestines. He studies my face for a negative reaction. I am not afraid. Satisfied, he continues finding exotic samples.

Nearby, a woman pushes a yellow cart decorated with painted letters spelling out "Kabayan." Painted red ribbons frame a hand drawn bowl of green and yellow balls.

Back in San Francisco, my Filipino friends told me detailed childhood stories of *sorbetes*, a brightly colored ice cream. They remember running out to the street when they heard a tinkle of the bells, signaling a nearby *sorbetes* cart. "It wasn't the best ice cream, but it was cheap, and I loved it," a friend relates. Dressed in a floral top and brown sandals, the woman gestures to her cart. I tiptoe to peer inside the yellow cart and motion to each of three canisters. Kelvin says, "This is what I thought ice cream only could be."

As she prepares a cone of mango, ube, and cheese, a nearby seller raises his eyebrows and says, "What are you doing?! Getting her *sorbetes* instead of your own ice cream?"

"When visitors are new to Manila, I want to show them everything!" Kelvin laughs, "Even when it's not my ice cream."

"I want to delight customers with a new flavor every week," Kelvin says as we end our day at his shop.

A group of three girls order a scoop of the Pop Rocks & mallows—a creamy ice cream folded with chocolate covered Pop Rocks and marshmallows. They each take a bite. Then one by one, they start giggling, and their faces fill with delight.

"I am grateful," Kelvin smiles, recalling the years since Merry Moo began. "Part of growing up is if you don't do it, no one else will."

Passion Fruit and Mango Ice Cream

2 cups whole milk

1 cup heavy cream

½ cup granulated sugar

4 egg yolks

Pulp from 7-8 whole passion fruit, including seeds (if not wrinkly, let the passion fruit sit in direct sunlight; after 8 hours, the passion fruit should be ripe)

1 whole mango

Combine milk, heavy cream, and sugar in a medium saucepan. Mix. Place over medium heat. When the mixture begins to simmer, remove from heat.

Whisk the egg yolks in a separate large bowl. Pour one cup of the warmed mixture into the bowl. Whisk immediately. Repeat two previous steps until less than a third of the warmed mixture remains in the medium saucepan. Pour the contents of the bowl into the saucepan. Place over medium heat. Stir frequently until the mixture thickens to a custard. Remove from heat when the mixture coats the back of a spoon.

Pour into a bowl. Stir the passion fruit pulp into the mixture. The seeds add texture to the ice cream. If that texture is not desired, strain out the seeds. Optionally reserve some pulp to serve after churning.

Chill for at least three hours or overnight in the refrigerator.

Slice up the mango into bite-size cubes. Set aside.

Scrape cold mixture into a pre-frozen ice-cream-maker bowl and churn according to manufacturer's instructions. Add cubed mango five minutes before churning completes.

Scoop ice cream into an empty resealable container. Freeze up to a month. To serve, let stand at room temperature until slightly softened, about 10 minutes.

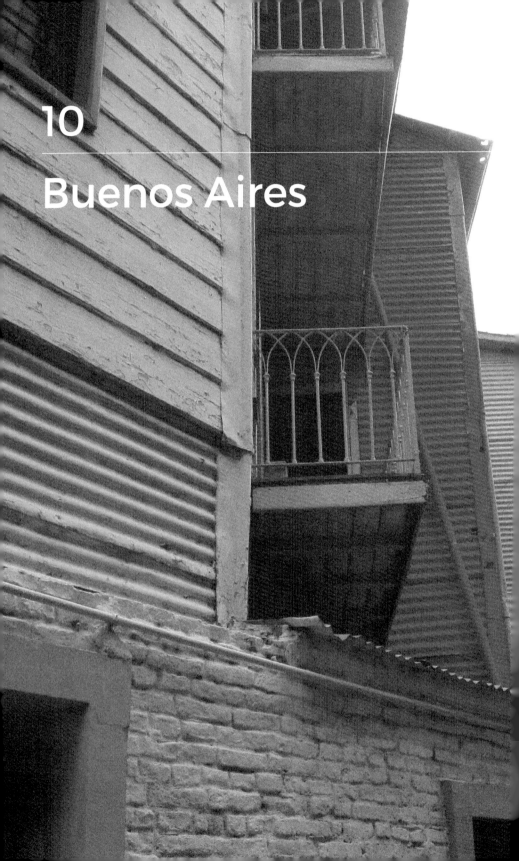

10

Buenos Aires

"Like Europe with a melancholic twist, Buenos Aires is unforgettable," Sandra Bao writes in a Lonely Planet travel guide to the city. The porteños—the city's residents or literally translated, people of the port—descend from Italian and Spanish immigrants, who brought their European culture to the country. Tango dominates the street, the sultry dance described as "making love while standing vertically." And the food: dulce de leche, caramelized milk, graces bread in the morning; Argentine ice cream, helado, more like its Italian cousin. Fresh meat grilled on parillas. To many of us, Buenos Aires is on the other side of the world—where their summers are our winters. Traveling to the "Paris of Southern America" from the Northern hemisphere can take over twenty-four hours.

The recession has led to economic fluctuation and political unrest. Broken sidewalks dot San Telmo, the oldest neighborhood in Buenos Aires. Yet in the upper-class Palermo, the old world charm persists with dazzling, classic architecture—vaulted ceilings, glass chandeliers—like strolling through cobblestone streets in Italy and Venice. But with the Argentine-accented Spanish, one remembers that this is Buenos Aires.

Locals love to recount their childhood. Rarely is there a porteño who does not recall regular visits to their neighborhood heladeria. This was the city that I was seeking—love of ice cream, endless hours spent in heladerias, and the deep connection between community and food. At a pool party, which lasted from the late afternoon until sunrise, porteños gossiped and invited us foreigners into their home. Helado was an easy topic. Tina ("like Tina Turner" she emphasized) kissed me twice on the cheek and said, "Everyone says that their neighborhood heladeria is the best."

Without a beat, Sofia described her relationship with helado, "I was seven years old when I discovered chocolate mint helado. I don't know how they did it, but they did it."

Another porteño advised, "Eat helado at midnight. It's the best way."

Unlike ice cream shops around the world, the heladerias in Buenos Aires stay open until 2 in the morning. A typical business day starts at 9 in the morning. Then porteños break for siesta from 1 to 4 in the afternoon. Dinner begins at 8:30 PM at the earliest. Then clubbing only begins at 1 in the morning. Heladerias fill up with a range of people throughout the day—children, individual businessmen, friends on break from shopping, a mother and a child after school. Helado is for all ages. Scooters with refrigerated trunks are a common sight in Buenos Aires, delivering a kilogram of helado to porteños' doorsteps.

Although many heladerias in Buenos Aires are national commercial chains—Un 'Altra Volta, Persicco, Freddo, there are few that are family-owned and artisanal. At Nonna Bianca, two flavors are handmade to reflect their electric taste—limon al pisco like the Peruvian pisco sour, and maté like the Argentine caffeine-infused drink served in a hollowed gourd. At Via Flaminia, a scooper says of heladerias, "It's worth going to a place for a certain flavor."

Damián Azrak, a blogger on the Helado Argentino, takes me on a tour of the heladerias in Buenos Aires. In his blog, he escapes from his day job of a lawyer and waxes on about his experiences with helado. He appoints himself the "helado police" and brings me on a tour of his favorite places. We stop by Rapa Nui, a shop from the Patagonia region with flavors like raspberry and chocolate, showcasing their artisanal chocolate making. Next is Jauja, a shop from the South with orange-tinted walls, showcasing flavors like cardamom and Oriental cream. Damián praises the quality of the dulce de leche and looks upward with each taste. Like all porteños, he says, "Nothing can stop me from having helado."

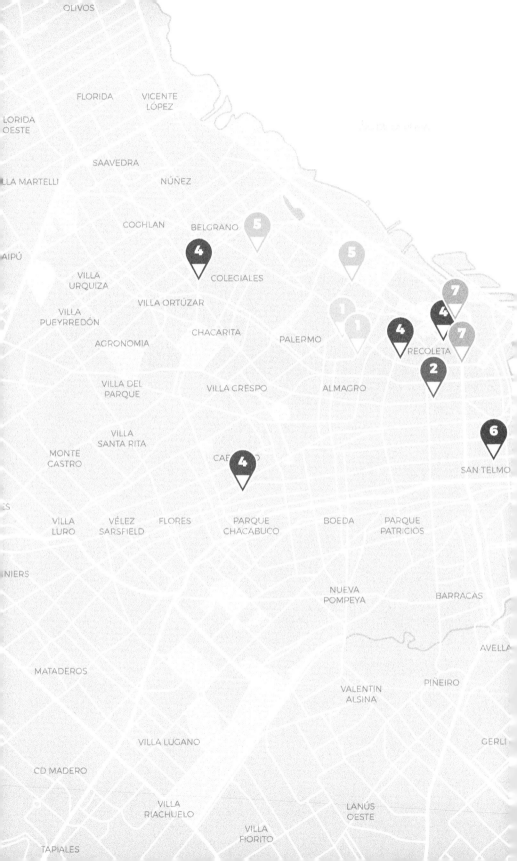

Heladeria Fratello ☆

heladeriafratello.com
+54 11 4821-2250
Av. Coronel Díaz 1521
Av. Medrano 1904

Heladeria Cadore ☆

heladeriacadore.com.ar
Av. Corrientes 1695
+54 11 4373-9797

A.M. Scannapieco

Av. Nazca 5274
+54 11 4587-8172

Rapa Nui

chocolatesrapanui.com.ar
0810-888-RAPA (7272)
Av. Elcano 3127
Arenales 2302
Av. Uruguay 1284
Av. Pedro Goyena 1515

Jauja

heladosjauja.com
Av. Federico Lacroze 2239
+54 11 4771-5978
Av. Cerviño 3901
+54 11 4801-8126

Nonna Bianca

Estados Unidos 425
+54 11 4362-0604

Arkakao

arkakao.com.ar
Av. Pres. Manuel Quintana 188
+54 11 4813-7585
Av. Santa Fe 1257
+54 11 4811-8802

Heladeria Fratello

Fratello, with two open-air locations in the Palermo neighborhood (and even one location in Barcelona, Spain), literally means "sibling" in Italian. Flavors like chocolate fratello (dark chocolate with orange peel and peach pulp) and sambayón tentación (chocolate buttons stuffed with dulce de leche) attract local families.

heladeriafratello.com

+54 11 4821-2250

Av. Coronel Díaz 1521

Av. Medrano 1904

Like in Italy, Argentines love to celebrate food with family and friends. Capturing that spirit, the helado shop Fratello—meaning brother in Italian—maintains tradition in their two open-air locations in the Palermo neighborhood in Buenos Aires. Lined with trees, its Parisian decor invites passersby to sit, relax, and have a small copa of helado.

My sister and I stumble across Fratello after a lunch at Cafe Nostalgia, a French bistro that lived up to its name, recalling a former era. Along the tree-lined street of Coronel Díaz and steps from a bustling five-way intersection, a ground to ceiling window showcases one Fratello location. A cool breeze flutters over the leafy trees. An oasis of leafy plants surrounds sidewalk tables and shelters the helado lovers from the streets. Around the shop's door, speckled tiles are faded from sunlight. One might wonder if this neighborhood was Paris with the boutique shops showcasing haute couture and European architecture, if not for Spanish flowing from pedestrians on their cell phones.

Inside Fratello, narrow signs list flavors in bold behind a counter. Chocolate lovers would rejoice on flavors like chocolate fratello (dark chocolate with orange peel and peach pulp) and sambayón tentación (an Argentine dessert flavor with chocolate buttons stuffed with dulce de leche). Sambayón, consisting of egg white and sweet wine, is the hardest flavor to make, but the owners insist on it to reflect the popular dessert custard. Flavors of dulce de leche, the Argentine caramelized milk, have a variety of mix-ins like brownies, chocolate chips, nuts, or bananas. There is also "simply super dulce de leche" meaning a dulce de leche helado marbled with dulce de leche.

While gazing at the flavors, a customer admits that she doesn't want helado, because it's too fattening. But within seconds, she forgets and orders a creamy flavor. A man uses a metal spade to scoop our selected flavors into a cone, twisting it to make a tall steady pyramid. My sister picks up an aqua-colored palettina, a small spoon used for helado. On its handle, the word "Fratello" is die cut. Like licking a spoon coated with dulce de leche, the dulce de leche granizado—the flavor with chocolate chips—oozes a deep buttery taste and ends with a milky finish. The namesake flavor Fratello is a vanilla cream helado broken up by chopped almonds and chocolate-dipped raisins, finished with a dash of rum. With little air, the dense helado highlights its origins. Real, whole ingredients are used here.

Within a ten-minute walk from Cafe Nostalgia, the second location of Fratello sits near a plaza. Yellow umbrellas shade tables. Here, palm trees stand above the opening. Inside the brick building, Diego Soto, the owner of Fratello, watches the shop fill with customers. Like a welcoming neighbor, he stands in front of the entrance. Diego waves us to join him. Like the other location on a dark green sign, the white letters "Fratello" are bookended by a red silhouette of palm trees. "Helados Artesanales Fratello" repeats on a narrow strip across the two display cases. Each flavor, like the dark green sign, is bookended with a red silhouette of palm trees. Each metal bin is sparsely decorated allowing the color and texture to speak for them. A mirror strip lies horizontally across all the interior walls, creating depth and space. Outside, a father watches as his daughter gobbles up a cone. Another woman places her shopping bag on the white chair and slowly licks her helado as she browses her mobile phone.

"Argentines have a lot of helado," Diego says. "Because of that ice cream in Argentina must be high quality."

Diego describes the quality of cream in Argentina and claims that it is best of the world. With ancestry from Italy, people in Argentina know how to cook, he says, and especially know how to make helado.

"Our main customers are local people, Argentines. Usually, when tourists come, it's because Argentines want to show them our ice cream. They are proud and want to share it. They want tourists or people

they know to taste it, because they know that it's good, right?"

The shop recently branched out to Barcelona in Spain. Unlike the two shops in Buenos Aires where helado is made at a factory, helado is made on site where customers can view into the kitchen, inviting them to show that there's nothing to hide. Argentines who visit Barcelona are pleased to find that their hometown favorite is good enough to be found in a foreign city. In Spain, Fratello, Diego says, is considered the representation of Argentine-style helado.

Tradition really matters to Diego. He wants to make helado like it always has been made. "Changes occur," Diego says. "New things come out, and we have to do it, because people ask for them since it's trendy. But we still sell the flavors that were popular 50 years ago. No matter what, people still crave the same taste of dulce de leche, sambayón, vanilla, and chocolate."

He is planning to make a flavor based on *pan dulce* or sweet bread, a traditional bread for Christmas. Shiny Christmas ornaments sparkle in the corner—a small green tree surrounded by ornaments and silver garlands. It is December now, and summer is reaching its peak in the southern hemisphere. Customers continue trickling into the store. Diego stands with his son, who has a dark brown mop of hair. Behind the counter, Diego cracks a smile each time he looks at his son. "My favorite time is when the children come," Diego says. "Children are happy when they eat helado, and I am very grateful for that."

"We are proud to make a family business of it, and we want to keep it that way," Diego says. "We are confident that the next generation will continue with this, and that makes us happy. It makes us feel proud, and gives us strength to work. That's Fratello."

Heladeria Cadore

Cadore, located at the busy intersection of Avenida Corrientes and Rodríguez Peña, intends to use the best ingredients for their customers. Italian immigrants from the town of Cadore, the shop's namesake, started the heladeria with extensive list of flavors from various dulce de leche flavors to South American fruits like passionfruit and tropical strawberry.

heladeriacadore.com.ar

Av. Corrientes 1695

+54 11 4373-9797

Hanging black and white photos explore the history of the shop. A family stands next to a large hand-cranked ice cream machine. A girl sits on a cart and watches her brothers while a man poses behind the cart. In another, a man wears dark pants, a white shirt, and a white messenger cap. One hand is on his hip, and another is resting on a cart with the letters "Cadore," referencing the Cadore region in northern Italy. Surrounded by the Alps, the Olivotti family handcrafted the frozen desserts for three generations. Cradling those same recipes, the family immigrated to Argentina and opened Cadore in Buenos Aires in 1957 on the corner of Avenida Corrientes and Rodríguez Peña. It was one of the first helado shops in Buenos Aires.

"We believe that ice cream of the future is actually ice cream from the past," says Gabrielle, a member of the current family generation running Cadore.

Silvestre is the grandson of the original founders of Cadore and still remembers arriving in Argentina in 1951 as a child and playing in the shop when it opened 8 years later. He walks with a slight stoop, and his thinning white hair is swept back. He manages the work during the night—the production of helado while Gabrielle manages the daytime operations. As we walk through Cadore, Silvestre places his hands on the machines and the tubs, holding them as if they were his offspring.

The Olivotti family made a choice. Unlike other shops in Buenos Aires today, helado is always made in the shop rather than at an offsite facility. They maintain an artisanal process, as they were in Italy, that they must keep the production and serving in the same place. Quality is not compromised.

Their standards are proven in the kitchen, where hulled, chopped strawberries float in an ice cream mixture. Taped to a machine is a handwritten list of today's flavors in blue cursive on white notepaper. Nearby, another machine pasteurizes the shop's cream mixture for at least twenty hours. In another pot, a mixture of milk, sugar, and vanilla cooks. "For fourteen hours over low heat," Gabrielle says when I peer over the lip of the pot.

Displayed next to an extensive list of flavors, family photos are backlit. Metal-trimmed chestnut wood serves as a backdrop to the words "Cadore" and "Gelato Artinginale." Below the menu and inside a sliding glass cabinet, upside down white cups and edible cones fill shelves in neat stacks, ready for a small appetite or a large appetite. Kilo tubs of helado are ready for delivery. A silver counter runs the length of the shop, broken up by deep wells, individual insulated metal containers with a lid—maintaining a unique temperature for each flavor. It's the traditional Italian way of storing the treat. Scoopers, adorned in white and mahogany uniforms, nod as a customer orders and reach for the lid of the desired flavor. Four men with dark hair and sun-tanned skin walk in, gossiping in Argentine Spanish, affected by decades of immigration from Italy. They prop themselves up on a metal bench along the counter. A small Christmas tree decked out with red spheres sits in a corner. A large photo of helado is printed on the awning as it shades the shop from the heat of December.

Outside, the Cadore awning blends in within the busy street of Avenida Corrientes, also known as "the street that never sleeps." On

the same street, Teatro Gran Rex and Teatro Opera, two multipurpose Art Deco theaters that house international acts, preserve history by serving as the cultural center of Argentina. A few miles away, the Obelisk rises as the icon of Buenos Aires. Matching the nickname of Avenida Corrientes, pedestrians rush past Cadore to work, or at night, to tango.

Tradition matters. The heladeria boasts an extensive list of flavors from various dulce de leche varieties to South American fruits like passion fruit and tropical strawberry. Bananas and mango come from nearby Brazil and Uruguay. Vanilla comes from Sri Lanka, Silvestre boasts. The watermelon flavor tastes like the flesh at its summer peak, and the lemon captures the fresh citrus taste as it lingers on my tongue. Gabrielle tells me about a special flavor for December–dulce de leche negro con chocolate a margo, or dulce de leche with dark chocolate. On my tongue, I first taste the sweet cream of dulce de leche. Then the nutty tang of the dark chocolate comes on the finish. "There's no rule in tastes," Gabrielle says. "There are people who like softer, stronger, and sweeter, with something inside to chew. Then there are people who want only helado."

Gabrielle laments about the state of helado. In Buenos Aires, chains of heladerias have pushed out most independent helado shops, with few like Cadore remaining. He and Silvestre glance at their current customers, all Argentines at the moment. They discuss how the bigger shops use flavored paste to distinguish the yellow cream from the white cream and chocolate cream. "We both put our heart in it, a lot of work, much effort to keep, to maintain. Because the main trend in the world is not to make this kind of helado," Gabrielle says. "We appreciate the tourists the most, because unlike the locals, they are not stuck in their hands. Tourists recognize quality when they see and taste helado."

"Because even the most humble people value the taste of ice cream," Silvestre says.

They pause for a second, thinking. The process to make helado at Cadore is time-intensive—days long—yet even after the industrialization of flavors and the number of smaller shops taking shortcuts, they resisted the temptation to do the same. I ask about their deep motivations. "I help girls asking questions." Gabrielle jokes looking at my sister and me.

We chuckle. Then his expression darkens, and he says, "To enjoy the passion to do things well and to know that on the other hand, there are people who value what I do."

Gabrielle opens the lid of a helado and swoops down with a spoon. "Here," he says. "Try this dulce de leche. It's incredible, and I think that you will find it too."

And he continues doing that. Over and over again.

Dulce de Leche Granizado Ice Cream

Stir half and half with ¼ cup granulated sugar in a medium saucepan over medium heat, until mixture starts to steam and bubbles start to form at sides of pan. Remove from heat.

Whisk egg yolks and remaining sugar in a large bowl. Wrap a damp kitchen towel around the base of the bowl (to prevent it from slipping). Gradually whisk in half of hot cream mixture. Return entire mixture to saucepan set over medium-low heat. Stir with wooden spoon constantly, until mixture is thick enough to coat the back of the spoon. Pour through a fine sieve into a metal bowl. Add dulce de leche and vanilla extract to the bowl. Mix well. Let stand for 10 min. Then lay plastic wrap directly on surface to prevent skin from forming.

Chill for at least three hours or overnight in the refrigerator. Scrape cold mixture into a pre-frozen ice-cream-maker bowl and churn according to manufacturer's instructions. Add chocolate pieces five minutes before churning completes.

Scoop ice cream into an empty resealable container. Freeze up to a month. To serve, let stand at room temperature until slightly softened, about 10 minutes. Serve as is. Feel free to add dulce de leche on top or other chocolate-ly goodness.

11

Istanbul

Travelers call it a city caught between the two worlds of the old and the modern. It is a cliché, but Istanbul is that city. It is steeped in not hundreds, but thousands of years of history—a Greek colony, then part of the Roman Empire, then the Ottoman Empire, and today the modern-day Turkey.

The Strait of Bosphorus splits the city into two—one on the European continent and the other on the Asian continent. The busy European side houses the city's treasures like Hagia Sofia and Topaki Palace and the chase scenes found in James Bond movies. Many residents live on the Asian or Anatolian eastern side, rarely ventured by tourists.

Mornings begin with the call of prayer projecting from the city's mosques. Like music, a gentle voice in Arabic floats above the rooftops. Platters of bread, cream cheese, and honey are paired with gold-rimmed glasses filled with deep brewed tea. Aromas of Armenian and Greek cooking waft from traditional rotating pits of beef. Flaky pastries layered with honey and pistachios peek from windows.

Along the streets, the Ustas (the masters) call weary pedestrians with jingles and spoons banging against metal canisters. It's time, they say, for some dondurma. A passerby stops, chuckles a bit, and signals the Usta for a scoop. The Usta hands the passerby a cone with a scoop and suddenly pulls it back with the spoon. It is gone, but then it reappears in the Usta's hand. Then the cone appears in the passerby's pocket and then moments later, gently pressed in the passerby's hands with multiple scoops. The show is for the tourists, and all ice cream lovers tell me about it. I see the same act in Danshui, a fishing village in Taiwan, transformed for global visitors. Yet in Turkey, the true ice cream aficionados dismiss the dondurma, a sticky concoction made of artificial ingredients. The artisanal Ustas tell me about their experiences in Italy and how to do gelato just right.

Girandola Dondurma

girandola.com.tr

Bebek Arnavutköy Cad. No: 109

    Arnavutköy

    Beşiktaş

    +90 212 265 2629

Caddebostan, İskele Sok. No:14

    Kadıköy

    +90 216 385 3666

Yaşar Ustanın Dondurması

dondurmaciyasarusta.com

Prof. Dr. Ali Nihat Tarlan Cad. No: 34/2

    Bostancı

    Kadıköy

    +90 212 325 3864

Dondurması Ali Usta

Moda Cad. No:264/A

    Kadıköy

    +90 216 4141880

Girandola Dondurma

Girandola, in the seaside neighborhood of Beşiktaş, started as a woman's dream to break away from Turkish ice cream and traditional gender roles. Inspired by Italian gelato, Girandola uses local produce like watermelon and grape to create refreshing gelato during the warm months along the Bosphorus strait.

girandola.com.tr

Bebek Arnavutköy Cad. No: 109

Arnavutköy

Beşiktaş

+90 212 265 2629

Caddebostan, İskele Sok. No:14

Kadıköy

+90 216 385 3666

"Girandola means 'kid toys'," Aslı says, trying to find the English words to explain what *girandola*, the shop's name, means in English. She's the chef and innovator of the couple-owned shop. Girandola is located in the Arnavutköy neighborhood, a former fishing village. A flowing circle of colors—pink, green, yellow, and orange—swirls on the deep blue awning and repeats throughout the open-air shop.

The translation of "girandola" eludes me. I Google it. Images of spinning lights appear in a grid. Fireworks? A special candle? Google indicates that it's an Italian word, but I am in Turkey. Four weeks later after meeting Aslı, a cyclist points to a pinwheel on his bike. "Kids love this," he says. "It's fun!"

The shop does embody fun. Whether "girandola" means a pinwheel, a handheld sparkly firework, or a large wooden spinning platform of elegant lights, Girandola beckons passerby to taste its array of delights. In the glass display, the flavors range from watermelon to cinnamon with caramelized apple and raisins to sour cherry. Aslı's eyes light up as she describes her flavors. Rose with poppy seeds. Chocolate. Raspberry sage. "Even mocha chocolate!" she exclaims.

"Mojito?" I offer, wondering about its origin.

As a lover of citrus fruits, the mojito flavor calls to me. The pale green sparkles, alluding to the layers of sweet and sour. But the word "fake" is awkwardly written in English on the label. Aslı frowns in sorrow. In Turkey, alcohol consumption is among the lowest in Europe—a result of a Muslim belief that alcohol promotes salacious acts. Even rakı, a traditional Turkish anise-seed-based drink, is no longer allowed in the country. In early 2013, the government tightened its laws in response to demands from citizens. Aslı bragged about her experimentation in alcohol before the ban. Why not use Jim Beam whiskey instead of rum? She loved how the whiskey changes flavors. But the changes stunt her creativity. "I want to make mascarpone and pear poached with red wine," she says. "They forbid us to have alcohol in ice cream. Before, the government allowed us 1.2% alcohol. Now it's zero."

She dreams of flavors that are not possible now: beer sorbet, cucumber with vodka, chocolate with Jim Beam, grapefruit with Campari, Italian desserts laced with liqueur. "I used to make beer," she laments. "I used to make zabaglione. I used to make tiramisu."

In response, her friends helped her. A friend's Jewish grandmother grew a special fruit to get as close to the flavor of whiskey as possible. Ufuk, her husband and co-owner, says, "After the alcohol ban, we can only make 'fake' flavors. Even the fake is very real."

Ufuk and Aslı are a strong pair. She is the chef and innovator. Her words spill out in snippets of Portuguese, French, and Italian. Her brown hair is pulled back, and she feels like a mother, a protector of her gelato. A pale brown apron wraps around her. Ufuk handles most business matters. When Girandola first opened, he worked at the family business based in Ankara, the capital city of Turkey, 282 miles from Istanbul. As they speak, he leans almost to protect her and beams as his wife talks about her craft. "Initially, Girandola was part-time for me," Ufuk says. "But now after three years, it is 100% of my time. Full-time ice cream!"

"Because he is my husband, then he felt obligated," she smiles.

Ufuk was an architect, and Aslı was a civil engineer. Over the span of twenty years, she returned to the kitchen, experimenting with foods. And then there was ice cream. As a child, she found Turkish ice cream very sticky. On the streets of Istanbul, I found the same—ice cream vendors dressed in traditional garb tossing a large scoop of ice cream from one spoon to the other. Back and forth, the ice cream stretched. She found the ice cream to be heavy. Could it be better?

Intrigued, Aslı went to Italy to take a course at the Gelato University,

a school sponsored by the ice cream machine-making company Carpigiani. First at Bologna, then at Milan, she learned about the gelato craft. There, her eyes opened. With the instruction of two maestros, she learned technique and aesthetics. Over time, she crafted the gelato into something personal that spoke to her.

Thirteen months later, she and Ufuk opened Girandola in 2007. Customers slowly trickled in to taste the hand-crafted gelato. "All my friends now knew that I was an ice cream chef," Aslı said as she describes the beginning.

In 2008, they opened in the current location. The national newspaper declared in a headline that same year: "Girandola: The best ice cream in all of Turkey." Since then, Girandola always makes the list.

"After two months of the opening, the newspaper without our knowing, they came and just wrote about this," Ufuk says. "When

they published, there was a boom. We had only two people on staff. We didn't have the resources to serve the customers."

Around the corner, a famed fish restaurant serves perfectly grilled fish with a tossed Turkish salad. A fruit stand sells fresh mulberries and peaches. The shop opens onto a paved boardwalk. Painted blue flowers stretch across the white ceiling. A large mirror reflects behind the display case and waffle cones. At the foot of the display case, children's drawings show their love of ice cream in smiling faces and dogs hungering for cones. The customers are loyal. Then she smiles, "For special customers, we make special flavors for them."

Even Turkish celebrities do not shy from Girandola. Ayşe Ajda Pekkan, a popular singer, and Kıvanç Tatlıtuğ, a hunky actor, visit frequently. "The A-list!" Ufuk brags and gestures outside the shop. "This area is the crème of the crème. They prefer us."

Ufuk and Aslı emphasize two dates that changed Girandola. May 19th is a special holiday in Istanbul. On that holiday a few years ago, the national newspaper showcased their shop, and business boomed. Then there is the 24th of June. Ufuk chuckles as he remembers his birthday in 2007. "She wanted this machine. She wanted this. She wanted that. I told her that tomorrow is my birthday. If you want to give me a present, then you have to make ice cream."

So, she made lemon sorbet. That was her first flavor.

Yaşar Ustanın Dondurması

Yaşar Usta, an outdoor ice cream stand in Bostancı, is the dream of an orphaned ice cream lover who snuck into Italy to learn about ice cream as a teenager. Adhering to quality ingredients and maintaining community, the shop attracts locals for its preservative-free fruit ice cream.

dondurmaciyasarusta.com

Prof. Dr. Ali Nihat Tarlan Cad. No: 34/2

Bostancı

Kadıköy

+90 212 325 3864

Yaşar Carli does not worry. In the last few days, the customers at his ice cream shop have been chattering wildly about the protests at Taksim Square. Located on the main residential thoroughfare to the train station on Prof. Dr. Ali Nihat Tarlan Street, the shop invites pedestrians to stop for a brief moment. Like a neighborhood grandfather, Yaşar dresses in a modest purple button-down shirt and slacks. When he spots a familiar face, he waves with a smile. He watches young adults head to Beyoğlu with gas masks and large flags featuring Ataturk, the first president of Turkey. As the protestors return, he greets them, addressing them by name and offering a taste of ice cream, a bright contrast during their day.

I meet Yaşar on a summer evening initially without an interpreter. Yaşar is clean-shaven, and a light blush emerges from his cheeks. As a devout Muslim, he just finished the fast for the preparation of Ramadan. Energy radiates from his eyes. Seeing an unfamiliar face, he becomes excited. Noticing me, Yaşar rises up from his chair behind the counter. His graying hair frames his rosy face as he approaches me, exclaiming greetings in all the languages that he knows. As I hand him hastily written Turkish on a piece of paper, his smile grows wider. Yaşar motions me over to the sign. The sign blares unapologetically "Yaşar Ustanin Dondurmasi" (in English, Master Yaşar, Ice Creamery, or as a friend notes later, Yaşar, Master of the Ice Cream Domain). Tapping a button, he flashes the colored lights on and off.

A young brunette scooper in a hairnet translates his words to basic English, "He is very happy! Love! Ice cream!"

I tiptoe and point at four pictures on the board: watermelon, honeydew, strawberry, and interestingly, a cow. No preservatives are found here. Everything is made fresh every morning. A young female scooper no more than twenty years old expertly scoops the ice cream into a cone. Yaşar motions me to go behind the metal counter. He opens the freezer, proudly displaying the colored bins. Then moving to a hidden bin, he plops a small scoop of orange colored ice cream on top of my cone. "Peach!" I exclaim as I take a lick.

My interpreter arrives, and Yaşar finally has a voice. He fills a table with fresh simit, circular bread with sesame seeds. Like a good Turkish host, he immediately serves black tea in small curved glasses, trimmed in gold. I drop a single cube of sugar and mix the tea with a small brass spoon.

Orphaned as a child, Yaşar lived on the streets of Bostancı, a neighborhood in the Asian side of Istanbul. Despite poverty, he searched for ice cream—to him, a small glimmer of happiness. With little education, he knew his opportunities in Istanbul were limited. Watching his friends fall into trouble, Yaşar became concerned. "I was scared to stay, but I was scared to leave everything I knew," he remembers. "Everyone thought I was crazy."

Armed with nothing but determination, Yaşar decided to follow his dream to Italy. Sneaking onto a cargo ship, he traveled through Bologna, Florence, and Rimini. There, he tasted all kinds of gelato. Soon, he found himself as an apprentice to a gelato maker. To his surprise, Yaşar discovered that the gelato was made with chemicals. "Why not just fruit and sugar?" he wondered. "Especially when that tastes better."

He entered gelato contests in Sicily and to everyone's surprise, he

started winning. His recipes were simple: fruit and sugar. Quality, he learned, was essential. Yaşar studied under other ice cream masters for nearly a decade.

Returning to his own neighborhood in Istanbul, he opened a shop in 1971 at an open-air movie theater. Closing the original shop in 1998, he decided to take a rest. Yet his customers still asked for him. With renewed energy, he opened the new shop in 2001 on the busy street.

"Every morning, I wake up at 4 AM. I go to the market and pick up the freshest fruits. People said that I was crazy that I would buy a kilo of blueberries for fifty liras and sell a kilo of blueberry ice cream for forty liras. But you see, people should always eat the good stuff."

Yaşar puts his hands together and exclaims, "Now, let's eat ice cream!" He scoops tahini ice cream onto a slice of bread. "This is my unique creation."

The taste of toasted sesame seeds slide down my throat. Its savory intensity melds quietly with the airy bread.

"I always eat half of kilo of ice cream in the morning," Yaşar says. "That way, I know that it's the best. You should not make your enemy eat something that you don't eat yourself."

His wife arrives and places her hand on his shoulder. She smiles.

Yaşar sits up and declares, "I feel embarrassed when I see ice cream makers who don't eat their ice cream. You see the five cupboards, there? Pick one. If you find something dirty, even an ant, I'll quit this job and close my shop. Let me tell you this: I believe that there are only three ingredients in ice cream: love, honesty, cleanliness."

I ask about the future.

Yaşar scans the faces of his young customers. He shakes his head and says, "Yaşar Usta doesn't desire for bigger things. When the goal is big, it loses its taste. One should have only one lover, if there are more than one, you cannot know the worth of them. One day, when these lovers start seeing others, you cannot control them."

The sky is dark now. Lights start flickering on in the residential neighborhood full of twelve-floor apartment buildings. Flags hang down from the balconies. The call for protests has quieted. Customers still line up for the ice cream. I ask about his best memories.

"Somewhere in 1968, the *Hürriyet* newspaper [the national Turkish newspaper] wrote a piece on my shop," Yaşar says. "'The first man in Turkey to make melon ice cream', it said! I never knew that they visited me."

Tears fill his eyes. He looks out at the busy neighborhood, his smiling customers, and his ice cream stand. "But today is my second best memory, when you came to hear my story."

Watermelon Mint Sorbet

Add watermelon chunks, sugar, lime juice, and tequila to a blender. If the all the chunks cannot fit all at once, blend a handful of chunks at a time. Puree the watermelon until there are no solid chunks left. Add mint to the mixture. Blend until the mint is thoroughly chopped and the leaves are blended throughout the mixture.

If blending in batches, use a large bowl to combine the batches. Add a pinch of sea salt and stir to combine.

For best results, chill the mixture for a few hours, although the mixture can be churned immediately if at room temperature or cooler. Scrape mixture into a pre-frozen ice-cream-maker bowl and churn according to manufacturer's instructions.

The sorbet is best served immediately. To store, scoop watermelon mint sorbet into an empty resealable container. Freeze up to a month. To serve, let stand at room temperature until slightly softened, about 10 minutes.

Visiting the Carpigiani Gelato University and Museum

A two-story ice cream cone sits in the parking lot entrance. The faux ice cream is a swirl of colors—stripes of dusty pink, sunshine yellow, and leafy green. Surrounded by bucolic fields, the Gelato University and Museum is nondescript, housed in a white building that stretches multiple football fields. Valentina Righi, the vice president of communications, walks down a staircase into the entrance. Above are the offices of the Carpigiani. Further in the back lies the Gelato Museum. To the left, students in the Carpigiani white jackets sit in a lecture hall on their second day of class, learning about the needed requirements for gelato. In an adjacent kitchen, students in groups of four mix ice cream batches and pour into ready ice cream machines.

Located several miles from Bologna city center, the Gelato University invites students worldwide to take its courses. They choose between a short one-week basic course or the complete immersive five-week training. Opened in 2003, the Gelato University is a project of Carpigiani, a manufacturer of Italian gelato machines. The company aims to spread gelato culture throughout the world. Instructors come from gelato shops and food science backgrounds. Although courses are taught in 12 worldwide campuses such as Algeria and Brazil, students travel to the headquarters in Bologna from all over the world—United States, Canada, China, Sri Lanka, Argentina, Brazil, Australia, and of course, Italy. Worldwide, the courses total over 590 in 10 languages, equating to over 15,000 class days. United to deliver the best gelato, students learn how to make gelato and how to build a long-surviving business with a business plan and design for the shop. Here, they learn "gelato harmony", a skill in balancing fat and sugar, and the business of selling gelato.

The core of the university consists of the lecture room, which seats 30 students at a time, and a kitchen with at least five gelato machines. Like a warehouse, linoleum floor stretches across the primary rooms. Today, the Italian course is in session, and students approach the end of their first week. Speaking Italian, students hail from Argentina and the home country of Italy. Each student wears a white cap and a Carpigiani white chef's jacket with two columns of buttons. After a lecture, students head to the kitchen. Today, they are making two kinds of gelato. First, they must make stracciatella with chocolate, a milk-based gelato with lines of chocolate. Then they will make bacio—literally a "kiss"-flavored chocolate gelato folded with crunchy hazelnuts. Groups of students huddle together at each station. They line

up across a white wall showcasing images of gelato and the words "Gelato Culture, Gelato Business, Gelato Innovation, Gelato University".

An hour later, the students present their gelato in the display case. Gelato University instructor Gianpaolo Valli leads the classroom, tasting the variations of the *bacio*. His navy chef's jacket contrasts the sea of students in white. Some students have made a bonus gelato—a fruit-based flavor. They gather around the display case. The shorter students are on tiptoe as he judges the final results.

"Too sweet," he says after tasting one gelato doused with a magenta-colored puree.

"Look at this one, the chocolate isn't even folded with the fior di latte gelato," he says about the base milk-based gelato. "Every spoon a customer has of a gelato must have at least a bit of chocolate. This chocolate is just on the top."

Then he approaches a cream colored gelato devoid of any decoration. "Perfect," he says after smacking his lips. "But it doesn't attract me. And it won't attract customers."

Gianpaolo focuses on the technique with the students. Psychologically, the color must attract customers. Ingredients need to be sourced appropriately, and they must be balanced in the recipe. When making the gelato, it must be at the correct temperature. Even an experienced gelato artisan might spend two hours in gelato preparation. Gianpaolo emphasizes the importance of calculation in recipes.

We sit in the classroom as the student attempt another round of gelato. "It's important to stay in good balance," he says.

When asked how his students are doing, he winks and responds, "Beyond all expectations. The passion burning inside them makes them fly."

The students do fly. Gianpaolo remembers James Coleridge, one of his most diligent students and owns Bella Gelateria in Vancouver, Canada—"he's crazy!"

Outside, a gelato shop is open to the public. A tour group sits in rows of chairs. They take photos with iPads and cameras, capturing a woman describing the gelato process in German. She gestures at an easel, then to a gelato machine rolled out to the group. A gelato instructor rushes out to start the gelato churning. It's early summer now, and the group wears short sleeves. A man pushes his white seat near a large plastic cone topped with a dark chocolate swirl. Their arms are crossed, but soon they relax when the gelato spills out of the machine. The tourists are invited to try the gelato.

One by one, they approach the counter. The display case is a rainbow of color—there is a cream-colored gelato drizzled with berry compote, brownie bites folded into a yellow gelato, and an undecorated *melone* gelato or cantaloupe. Stacked cups sit next to teetering columns of upside down cones. A student greets them in English and offers samples. A creamy gelato is presented on a *palettina*, or a colored transparent spade. Curious, the tourist asks for more, tasting a light pink concoction of strawberries and milk. Then the gelato is scooped into a cup with the Carpigiani logo, its contents nearly spilling.

Students, who are in the advanced course, staff the gelato shop. Today, it's an English course, and students travel from a range of countries—United States, Canada, England, Sri Lanka, China. An American couple from the East Coast, Kerri and David, met while working for Homeland Security. Inspired by trips to Italy and a gelato maker in Louisiana who made similar gelato, they decided to change their lives to be gelato makers. It's the third week now, and the focus is on the chemistry of the gelato—the reaction of sugar with each gelato

ingredient. A young man in his twenties, urged by his father, takes the course so that he can work at his father's gelateria in Shenzhen, China. It is his goal to spread the love of gelato across Chinese communities. Another young man from Sri Lanka discusses his sister's passion in baking cupcakes. To complement her work, he wants to make gelato.

Then it's time for the Gelato Museum. We are in Italy, of course. The museum boasts about the Italians' success in the gelato making. "American ice cream is not the same," a guide says. "Italians figured out how to make great gelato."

An illustration of man mixing a concoction over fire, drawn in the 11th century, sits next to a printed description: "*Shrb*: sugar syrup, a base for making fruit sorbets, medical herbs, spices, flowers, and so on."

All over the globe, I have been unable to find a consistent story of the origin of ice cream. It's not Roman Emperor Nero sending his servants to the mountains. It's not the Chinese mixing milk with rice. Based on an Arab manuscript from the 11th century called *Book of Sorbets*, created ten centuries after the Roman Empire, that described the chilling and infusion of sugar mixtures placed into earthenware jars, here, ice cream and gelato originates from the *shrb*.

Old boxes that once held gelato protrude from the walls. "Cono Nordico" in red letters floats next to a drawing of a woman holding gelato on a cone. On one side of the box, *Fragilissimo* warns the transporter to care for the contents. The guide invites me to push a wooden paddle attached to a wooden barrel, demonstrating the first hand-cranked machines in Italy. Its wheel makes gelato churning easier. Black and white images capture the gelato makers in the early days: a man sells gelato and espresso, and another depicts a family pushcart labeled *gelati*. On display, a former working gelato Rube

Goldberg machine shows its inner workings—gelato cups move along a conveyer belt to collect gelato and dispense for 150 Italian lira or 90 US cents. Gelato molds hint at potential shapes like lamb, shells, fruit, and flowers.

Facts about the frozen dessert dominate the space. Francesco Procopio Cutò, originally from Sicily, opened the first ice cream shop, Café Procope in Paris. It exists to this day. Francesco Redi, a poet and physician from Arrezo, wrote about sorbet's impact on a young boy and his opinion on sorbets in his famous dithyramb "Bacchus in Tuscany"—a classical hymn honoring Dionysus, the god of wine:

Of jasmine

I don't make drinks

but I weave garlands

to wear on my head:...Sorbets are amber

and a thousand other scented waters

are drinks for lazy people...

Lorenzo Magalotti, a scholar hailing from Tuscany, formed the framework of the first recipe of gelato in the 1600s. In his account in *Del Candiero*, he describes gelato's ingredients—eggs, sugar, moss, amber, jasmine, lemons—and the "scrape and stir" mechanical action like the churning in today's machines.

Back then, gelato symbolized wealth. In English and Italian, printed quotes about gelato line the museum walls. Ippolito Nievo from Palermo, the capital city of Sicily, writes in *Garibaldi's Letters*, "We live in the royal palace. We get gelato as big as steak."

The tour ends, and the guides insist on taking a photo of me near a white Gelato University sign. I stand there, and smile. I have found gelato.

12

Bologna

The red city. *La Grasa*, the fat one. These are nicknames of Bologna.

Bologna is my first stop in Italy. The roads are paved with cobblestones. Ancient gates of stone, once barring outsiders, stand reflecting history. The leaning towers of Bologna, still red, recall families outdoing each other in the 1100s. One of the longest arcades in the world, the Portico of San Luca, brings a visitor from the center of the city to view it from the outside, showcasing Bologna and its architecture.

Today, Bologna is a university town, attracting thousands of students. English speakers pepper the population. Tourists arrive for the Emilina Romaggnia regional food—the Bolognese sauce and the ravioli. A friend leads me to a stand selling tortellini al brodo, filled pasta in light stock. Young locals, dressed in red capes and handmade Roman hats, organize a flash mob imitating Napoleon. Outside the city lies the Carpigiani factory, which houses the Gelato University and Gelato Museum.

Then there's the gelato. Quality gelato has certain characteristics. Food bloggers remind visitors not to have overly decorative gelato shaped in "mounds". Yet an American ice cream maker boasted about imported ingredients for his gelato, "These cans are filled with authentic Italian syrups."

His ice cream was good, but I puzzled over the gelato. Wouldn't great gelato be made out of fresh strawberries and toasted pistachios? I learn that is the truth. As I later walk through a gelato festival in Florence, the producers of the syrups and the milk powder are the foundation of industrialized gelato. It is cheaper, but it's not higher quality. The gelateria maestros I selected emphasize *gelato artigianale,* or artisanal gelato. They use local ingredients, and what a gelato maker called "the American way." They are unafraid of challenging the culture—using quality ingredients and showcasing the production. This, I discover, is proof that the *gelato artiginale* culture started here.

PESCAROLA

LAME

BOLOGNINA

SAN DONNINO

PILASTRO

SAN DONATO

SCANDELLARA

GHETTO
EBRAICO

CIRENAICA

CROCE
BIACC

BARCA

VILLA
GHIGI

GIARDINI
MARGHERITA

SAN LAZZA
DI SAVENA

VILLA
RIZZI

PONTICELLA

MARTIDI D

Gelateria Sole Luna

gelatodicapra.it

Via Riva di Reno, 7

   +39 346 857 0085

Gelateria Stefino Bio

stefino.it

Via S Vitale, 37

   +39 051 587 4331

Cremeria Scirocco

cremeriascirocco.it

Via Agostino Barelli, 1

   +39 051 601 0051

La Sorbetteria Castiglione

www.lasorbetteria.it

Via Castiglione, 44 d/e

   +39 051 233257

Gelateria Sole Luna

Sole Luna, located near the city center, is everyone's dream of ice cream, quality ingredients while fitting many dietary restrictions. The gelateria considers all diets. Made from goat milk, flavors are nut-free and gluten-free.

gelatodicapra.it

Via Riva di Reno, 7

+39 346 857 0085

"I can't have milk," says a man.

"My boy is allergic to strawberries," says a woman.

"I don't want to get fat," another adds and then turns to me. "It would be horrible if you were lactose intolerant."

I chuckle and admit that I am lactose intolerant. A little. Yet not when it comes to quality ice cream. It might be the way that it is crafted. I assure fellow guests at a friend's party back in San Francisco that everybody can have ice cream. "Delicious ice cream," I say. "Nobody needs to be denied it."

Gelateria Sole Luna, located on the borders of Bologna, embodies that dream—,made from goat milk, with flavors that are nut-free and gluten-free. Located across from a gym, Bologna gelato lovers flock here without guilt. Some twice a week. Some come almost every day. "This gelato has low amount of fats compared to normal gelato," says De Munari Wassilli, the owner of Sole Luna. "Definitely."

My colleague and I arrive early in the morning. Sole Luna is nestled in a residential neighborhood. The edge of a garage door hangs above us. Two photos of children eating gelato suggest that families flock here. This gelateria is my first interview in Italy, and I approach with excitement. As I move closer, I hear the familiar hum of a display case, a freezer working to maintain cold temperatures. De Munari pops up behind the glass display cases. He has been making fresh gelato for three hours in preparation for opening. Thirteen flavors in those hours, he tells us later. Some days sixteen flavors. Dressed in white topped with a white cap, his cheeks are flushed. Despite working as a chef nonstop since he was eighteen, he bounds toward us with youthful energy. He has worked internationally—in Egypt, Malta, France, Greece—crafting Italian cuisine like pastries and cakes. Sole Luna is his dream and embodiment of his philosophy. Gelato is never more than two days old, and the machines constantly churn new batches. De Munari waves his hands over his work behind the counter, gelato mounds shaped for the masses. "Please come back!" he says. "Please, I want to make it perfect for you."

My colleague brings me to a nearby cafe to experience an Italian breakfast: a pastry and a coffee. "Every day: coffee," a Bologna local tells me later. "And every day: gelato."

De Munari opened his first gelateria in the village of Monteveglio, also named Sole Luna, in 2006. After working as a chef for eight years, he wanted a change—crafting delightful tastes for food lovers. He trained at the Carpigiani's Gelato University for the basic techniques in a two-day course. "It's a learning by doing job," De Munari says.

Like many gelato makers, De Munari started making gelato with cow milk and flavoring syrups. But, inspired by the nearby farms, he decided to use the goat milk. People fell in love the taste. The goat milk gelato contains no food coloring, no preservatives, and no cream. He incorporated more natural products from farms, decreasing artificial ingredients little by little in the gelato. In pursuit of low-sugar gelato, De Munari replaced the sweet ingredient with honey. He describes his rebalanced recipe for *fior di latte* gelato, which celebrates the combination milk and cream—"a tiny bit of sugar helps balance the flavor" so that the taste isn't overpowered by honey. His aims to lower fat, despite the "rule" that fat makes gelato creamier. "I could find other natural substitutes and get the same results," he says.

It was not easy. "People would think I was out of my mind doing something different from the typical gelateria, using a different type of milk," De Munari remembers. "People thought it was too risky."

People believed that goat milk would taste sharp and increase costs. Because goat milk gelato does not require cream, the gelato prices at

Sole Luna match the price at other gelaterias. The gelateria attracts ardent followers. "They are mostly celiac, lactose intolerants, or people with different food intolerances, like cocoa intolerants and so on," he says. "But I also get common people as usual customers. Very few gelaterias are like us in all of Italy."

Dairy-free gelaterias like Sole Luna are rare: two in Northern Italy, another on the island of Sardinia, and another in Southern Italy. De Munari met a woman whose son was allergic to cocoa. She suggested using carob. To his surprise, the carob gelato strongly resonated with his customers. On the tongue, its brown texture melts into a whirlpool of layers recalling cocoa and toffee. "I could never get rid of it," he says and smiles.

"I am allergic to many things," De Munari admits. "When I was a child, I could only eat *ghiacciolo*. There's no milk in it; just water and sugar."

Ghiacciolo is a popsicle, frozen flavored ice circling a wooden stick, nothing like ice cream or gelato. It's different for De Munari now. "I eat the gelato I make!" he says.

He moved the gelateria to Bologna in March 2013 to be closer to his customers. De Munari's well-connected friend invited the movers and shakers of Bologna to the opening. They blocked traffic. "Around 500 people showed up in the end!" De Munari recalls and claps his hands in delight. "There were all different sorts of people, like comedians and famous people who work in TV."

De Munari gestures to the machines where he creates his famous gelato. He makes two base mixtures—a *fior di latte*, a clean vanilla-like flavor, and *crema*, which celebrate the intoxicating richness of egg yolks. With the *fior di latte* base, he makes hazelnut, pistachio, chocolate, and many others. With the *crema* base, he makes custard-based gelato.

De Munari recommends the yogurt flavor. I taste richness full of tartness and creaminess. I love the way it trickles down my tongue without feeling sticky. Unlike my first cup of gelato in Italy the previous night, this gelato is light, and I don't feel its sweetness weighing me. Unlike gelato made with cow milk, Sole Luna's yogurt gelato is sour, like a squirt of a lemon, as it rolls across my tongue and ends with a sweet finish.

"I hope I'll be happier than this in the future," he continues. "I'd like to have 3 or 4 gelaterias all over the world. I only want to have one in Italy, no more."

La Sorbetteria Castiglione

La Sorbetteria is the first gelateria in Italy to unleash the secrets of gelato making. Customers can view the fresh produce, the pasteurization, and the churning in the laboratorio. Famous for fruit flavors, the first La Sorbetteria is located in an affluent neighborhood lined with offices and high-end fashion.

www.lasorbetteria.it

Via Castiglione, 44 d/e

+39 051 233257

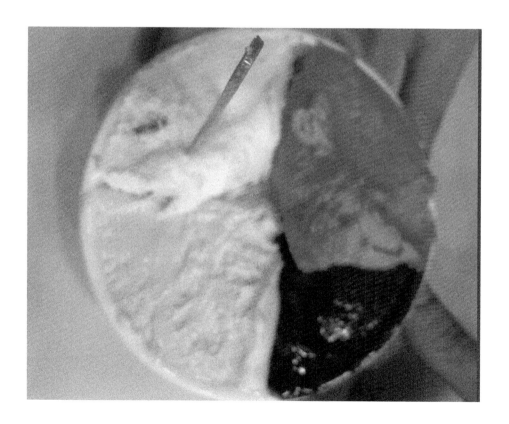

"It was freezing outside," a California gelato maker said of a winter visit to Bologna. "But they opened their doors and invited us in. It was the most amazing gelato."

She and her husband were not the only people enraptured by Giacomo Schiavon's gelato at La Sorbetteria. Even in Canada, where I met another gelato maker who proclaimed that his gelateria was the best in North America, I asked about gelaterias that he admired. "La Sorbetteria in Bologna," he responded.

By the time I reached Italy, I had tasted a range of flavors, and discovered what I loved most was simplicity. Fruit grown on local farms—a celebration of the community. Lemons. Peaches. Berries. Strawberries, especially.

"Chocolate!" my friend from Bologna exclaims. "You must have chocolate."

So I do. The chocolate gelato is smooth, like a cold chocolate bar. Flavors are named after Giacomo's children—Crema Michelangelo, a praline almond; Crema Edoardo, mascarpone with caramelized pine nuts that emulates a nutty cheesecake; Dolce Karin, a mixture of white chocolate and hazelnut. Pastries beckon us, with fruit folded in buttery dough. This is the work of Marina, the wife of Giacomo, a pastry genius who creates sweet bread pairings with gelato.

We are in an affluent neighborhood of Bologna—lawyers and doctors live in the above apartments, and high-end shops populate the street of Castiglione. La Sorbetteria is the highlight. The name in script is scrawled across the big windows to welcome us. Three vertical gelato machines rise above the counters, framing a sweeping view of the production—an expansive metal table, pasteurizer, the blast freezers, and a pallet of ingredients. Fresh milk. Fresh cream. Ricotta. Mascarpone. Sugar. This view, I discover, is rare in gelaterias. In Florence, doors marked "do not enter" bar me from asking questions about the gelato. *It's a secret*, gelato makers tell me, *what you see here is everything*.

But Giacomo believes in something more revolutionary. Originally from a medieval Sicilian village facing the Eolie Islands, he brought to Bologna the Sicilian traditions of pastries and granita. He started out in an established gelateria, but when the owners sold, the standards

lowered in quality. Disappointed, he needed to make a choice—to take advantage of his electrical engineering education or become a chef. Out of passion, he pursued gelato. With his wife's help, he designed La Sorbetteria, to address the gap between quality and gelato. At the time, Bologna was known for tortellini and cakes. The doors of La Sorbetteria opened in 1994, and Bologna, in under a decade, became a flagship city in Italy for gelato.

La Sorbetteria does not display mounds of finished gelato. Rather, each flavor is stored inside small metal containers to maintain the ideal temperature. "Before I started my company 90% of gelaterias had open display freezers," Giacomo says. "If you open it, the temperature will change, and the gelato is affected. Open display freezers need defrosting every few hours, so it will have no power for twenty minutes, causing the gelato to melt and refreeze. So you get big pieces of ice in the gelato. Ice bits in gelato must be small to make gelato creamy, but if it melts and freezes many times, this is not possible."

Yet Giacomo understands visual appeal. "This is why we have an open kitchen, for people to see everything in the making. Here you can see the process while the chef transforms ice cream from liquid into solid. Sometimes it is difficult to see all of the process and understand it. It is beautiful to watch, but you need explanation. There are no secrets here. Well, for the recipes, but not for our process and ingredients."

Although La Sorbetteria has permits to make cooked food, 80% of the focus is on the gelato. The other 20% is dedicated to how baked goods can support the gelato like La Sorbetteria's take on Christmas panettone, a traditional Italian sweet bread, surrounded by gelato. La Sorbetteria lovers flock here not to cool down, but for a sweet treat. This change of perception elevates the gelateria. "We transformed ice cream into dessert," he says. "If you want to sell it all year long, you have to serve it as a dessert as well. If you want to sell cold ice cream then it would be a product sold exclusively in the summer."

La Sorbetteria celebrates the summer and its namesake with sixteen different types of *sorbetto*, a fruit and ice mixture, which tends to be colder and far sweeter than gelato. But people flock for the gelato year-round. In Bologna, Giacomo tells us, people have gelato all day like espresso, because their gelato is not too sweet.

Dessert and passion are the key words. What aspiring gelato makers

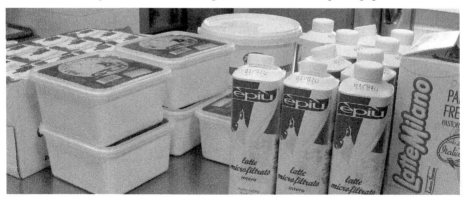

don't know is that long hours are typical—oversight is needed for consistent gelato and attentive customer service. It's not a profitable job. According to Giacomo, 30% of gelaterias closed during the first year of business due to mismatched expectations. "People think that they will work less making gelato," Giacomo says. "As if spending 12 hours in the kitchen is a lot of fun. It's a misconception. If they have no passion, then they become frustrated with customers too."

A calculator sits on the metal table. Through 11 years of development, Giacomo developed a digital program that generates recipes that maintain gelato creaminess while decreasing the amount of sugar. With the program, he avoids iciness that occurs with low sugar amount. He describes the requisite ingredient of air, which enters gelato via milk proteins and the bases for gelato. Giacomo has created fifteen individual mixtures of milk, cream, and egg yolk. A base is selected for how well it can enhance the other flavors in the recipe.

The pistachios come from Bronte in Sicily. He shells the nuts, then grinds and toasts them himself, letting the natural oils flavor the gelato. Three different types of cocoa are used in chocolate gelato. Giacomo points at the milk on the counter and says, "To you, this is milk. Not to me. This is a product with 35 grams of fat, 20 grams of lactose, and water."

Flavors at La Sorbetteria awaken childhood memories. Tasting the gelato, I visit the "old world" of Italy. First, the light yellow Crema Bolognese—the taste is reminiscent of the egg custard used for traditional cakes that Italians ate as children. Then the Sicilian Cassata. For Giacomo, it recalls the Cassata Siciliana, a traditional cake from Sicily surrounded by colored fruit jellies. The jellies are absent of course, yet the gelato recalls sponge cake infused with fruit liqueur and ricotta. Torta degli Addobbi, a sweet rice cake made in Bologna for celebrations, inspired a flavor consisting of lemons and amaretto.

"I remember my grandma and her famous pasta and cakes," Giacomo says. "I remember her Sunday lunches. She gave us fresh ricotta and caramelized figs, a typical Bolognese menu. The fresh ricotta came not from the store but from local farmers. Plus, she grew her own figs."

I taste the strawberry gelato. By my request, of course. It is of Giacomo's dreams. A dessert, but not too sweet. And it's like eating a ripe, fresh strawberry.

Blood Orange Sorbet with Candied Peels

If making candied orange peel, peel the oranges to desired strips, removing as much of the pith as possible.

Remove peels from any remaining oranges.

Juice the oranges. Ideally, a juicer works best. However, a blender works well to "juice" the blood oranges. If using a blender, remove all seeds by hand. Blend the fruit to get approximately 3 cups of blood orange juice and pulp.

Place 1 cup of blood orange juice in a small saucepan over medium heat. Stir in the sugar and zest until dissolved. Let cool and blend the blood orange sugar syrup with the remaining blood orange juice.

Chill the mixture at least three hours or overnight in a refrigerator.

Scrape cold mixture into a pre-frozen ice-cream-maker bowl and churn according to manufacturer's instructions. Freeze up to a month. To serve, let stand at room temperature until slightly softened, about 10 minutes. Serve as is, or with candied orange peels.

Optional candied orange peel

Peels from the blood oranges   3 cups sugar

Cut the peels into at least ¼ inch width strips. These can be chunky or long curly strips, depending on preference.

Cover the strips with water in a medium saucepan. Bring to boil over high heat and boil about 15 minutes. Drain. Repeat. If the strips contain pith, repeat once more. Drain.

In the saucepan, combine 2 cups of sugar and 1 cup of water. Bring to a boil until the mixture reaches thread stage, which is approximately 230 degrees or when a drop of the sugar water in cold water forms a thread. Add the peels and stir. Lower the heat and simmer for about 5 minutes. Drain.

Cool the strips on a wire rack. When cool enough to handle, roll strips in the remaining sugar until thoroughly coated. Let dry on a wire rack overnight. Strips can also be kept in an airtight container for a few months.

13

Rome

The hardest part of visiting Italy is to stop thinking that it's not a dream. That the Roman columns, the carved stone . . . this is where history happened. The structures were built centuries ago in an ancient era. Growing up in the United States, a young country, the aged look is an added design aesthetic. In trendy American restaurants, exposed rafters exude a vintage, old-fashioned feel. But in Italy, the same look has been present for generations. The rolling hills of Italy match temperate California weather. Roman farmers markets radiate the similar enthusiasm as the San Francisco Bay Area farmers markets with fresh produce and artisanal baked goods. I ask my host, "Would you move anywhere else?"

"I would, yes, [since] there's better opportunities elsewhere," she begins. "But I love the weather here. How can I live anywhere else?"

Rome is a city of layers. Literally. In 2014, a third of the planned subway had been built, halted by archaeological digs along the route. The magic of Rome lies in its history. In high school, European History encompassed events that held little interest for me. Fifteen years later, I discovered that Rome contained more than facts in textbooks. Expats led me to cozy dinners in the alleyways of Trastevere, late night snacks of *arancini* or fried rice balls, and nighttime strolls past the Colosseum. We rode on scooters around the city, dodging traffic and whizzing past landmarks. Rome is a city of boisterous rule and sweeping symbols of art.

Following my love of film, I touched the water of Trevi Fountain as in *La Dolce Vita*, visited the scene of the chase to the Church of Santa Maria del Popolo in *Angels and Demons*, and hiked through the Colosseum, a spotlight of its own. As for gelato, only one scene matters: sitting on the Spanish Steps with a gelato in hand and gazing into the space simulating the scene where Gregory Peck "accidentally" runs into Audrey Hepburn in *Roman Holiday*.

The best gelaterias are unknown, hidden from the historical center of the Pantheon and Piazza. Yes, guidebooks highlight the famous Gelateria San Crispino and Palazzo del Freddo Fassi, but the rising stars of gelato are, like the great food in Italy, located elsewhere. They are tucked into dead-end alleyways and hidden beneath apartment buildings. Yet it is in Rome where the gelateria maestros speak about their gelato so much like the chefs of Michelin three-star restaurants. The quality, the ingredients, and the process matter.

A local English-speaking tour guide, Simona, from Walks of Italy urges me to ask cab drivers about their favorite gelato. "Fassi," one says.

She tells me that most Romans are unaware of where to get quality gelato, because the artisinal gelaterias appeal to those who care. These gelaterias use natural ingredients to break away from industrialization—the syrups and powders produced by a well-respected company. But it's difficult. Family values hold strong in Italy where the older generations are revered for their wisdom and experience. Starting a new business is rare, unless backed by family or community. Mainstream Romans are unaware of the gelato made from natural, whole ingredients.

I had gelato every day, walking along the water of the Tiber River with a mini spoon dipping into my treat, stepping carefully over the cobblestones. Fatamorgana had flavors named after fairy tales like Punch Paradise (Terracina strawberries, white wine, and lemon) and Snow White (Tahitian vanilla, apple, and raspberry sauce). Otaleg!—gelato spells backwards—turns traditional gelaterias by 180 degrees by showing its Cattabriga gelato machine first rather than the gelato. No matter where I go, I have my gelato. By the cup, not the cone, as some gelateria makers instructed me. "It's the purest way," one says. "Without the cone intruding on the taste."

I loved it all.

Fatamorgana

gelateriafatamorgana.it

Via Lago di Lesina, 9

  +39 06 8639 1589

Via Giovanni Bettolo, 7,

  +39 0637519093

Via Laurina, 10

  +39 0632652238

Via Roma Libera, 11 (Piazza San Cosimato)

  +39 06 580 3615

Piazza degli Zingari, 5

  +39 06 4890 6955

Via Aosta, 3

  +39 06 7030 6848

Gelateria del Teatro

gelateriadelteatro.it

+39 06 4547 4880

Via dei Coronari, 65

Lungotevere dei Vallati, 27

Il Gelato di Claudio Torce

ilgelatodiclaudiotorce.com

+39 06 9788 2939

Via dell'Aeronautica, 105

Via Aventino, 59

Via Stoccolma, 7

Fior di Luna

fiordiluna.com

Via della Lungaretta, 96

  +39 06 6456 1314

Gelateria di Gracchi

gelateriadeigracchi.it

Via dei Gracchi, 272

  +39 06 321 6668

Otaleg!

otaleg.com

Via dei Colli Portuensi, 594

  +39 338 651 5450

Palazzo del Freddo di Giovanni Fassi

palazzodelfreddo.it

Via Principe Eugenio, 65

  +39 06 446 4740

Settimo Gelo

Via Vodice, 21/A, 00195 Roma, Italy

alsettimogelo.it

+39 06 372 5567

Il Gelato di Claudio Torce

Il Gelato is the most innovative gelateria in Rome and engage disciples with simple classic flavors to experimental flavors like bell pepper and mushroom. With various locations throughout Rome, his primary gelateria is in EUR, a quiet leafy neighborhood outside the city center.

ilgelatodiclaudiotorce.com

+39 06 9788 2939

Via dell'Aeronautica, 105

Via Aventino, 59

Via Stoccolma, 7

My colleague and I apologize via text message to Claudio Torce as we fly across Rome in a taxi. That is, as much as we can fly through congested roads to EUR, a quiet leafy neighborhood located on the outskirts of Rome. Although other franchises of Il Gelato lie close to the city center, his flagship gelateria is here in EUR. Earlier, a subway official waved his hands, telling my colleague and me in cautionary Italian that the next train was not arriving. "That's Rome," Claudio responds within seconds.

He meets us at the door, smoking a cigarette and dressed in a polo shirt. The gelateria is at the foot of a tall building. Claudio towers at his height of six feet. His quiet demeanor becomes apparent as he smiles and leads us to the sunny garden next to Il Gelato. The logo is simple—a yellow circle encases "il gelato" and a yellow square. Claudio's name is not even listed; it's evidence of his modesty.

Speaking in quiet Italian, he explains his desire to spend all day in his laboratorio. He imagines unusual flavors—perhaps the Italian dish of *melanzane alla parmigiana* or eggplant parmesan. Following the classic recipe for the dish and then extracting the flavors, he adds the milk, cream, and sugar to turn it to gelato. "The best thing is the laboratorio," he says. "I love being there, so I've been delegating the selling to others. That way, I can stay in the laboratorio and play!"

He hesitates mid-sentence. Claudio is self-conscious and glances around the garden at his customers enjoying gelato. "You cannot imagine my embarrassment, being in front of you," he says. "The worst day of my life was an interview for an Italian television show, *Gusto*. So painful. I feel good only inside my laboratorio. I love touching and smelling aromas, ingredients, and gelato flavors. I love playing with all of this."

Flavors are his "babies". Chocolate and pistachio are the favorite flavors of customers. So Claudio presents those flavors' variations first in the display case. Zabaione is his "first baby", a flavor recalling the south Italian dessert made of eggs, sugar, and Marsala wine. Its recipe hasn't changed since the shop opened in 1993. There's the strawberry, my personal favorite, which sparkles on my tongue. "You'll taste it," he says. "Then its taste disappears, and you'll feel memories rising. You'll see."

The savory flavors are in the back, furthest away from the front door. Claudio nods. "It's like a punishment," he says.

He doesn't want to scare locals with flavors like tomato soup and mushroom, yet a devilish glint appears when he talks about his experiments. Claudio dips a tasting spoon into the onion frittata gelato. The flavor is smooth, with aromas of fried eggs and caramelized onions. Then I try *puttanesca*, a flavor inspired by a pasta sauce made of tomatoes, olives, oil, garlic, and capers. The Sambuca gelato imitates the liquor at the end of the meal—leaving a finish of anise and coffee. Claudio giggles as he remembers a gelato of *baccalà alla vicentina*, salted codfish with cream and onion. Because onions were sautéed onsite, customers wrinkled their noses and cried, "What a smell!"

Claudio savors those moments when he surprises people. Before his shop became popular, he placed dry ice at the shop entrance to entice people with the swirling cloud. Mortadella gelato was the turning point and is today the only savory flavor displayed at the front of Il Gelato. Initially, visitors grinned and sniggered, but after declaring that the flavor was "horrible", they tasted other flavors. "It made me stand out among all other gelato makers," Claudio recalls. "It is difficult to convince people to try new flavors. I think that the reason is that gelato has 2,700 years of history. But it's also 2,700 years of dust and cobwebs."

Yet, for Claudio, it's that tradition that led him to gelato. His love of sweets and experimentation runs in his family. His grandfather

originated from a town in the Tuscany region known for pastry chefs, and in 1930, he opened a *patisserie* and *pizzeria*. After high school and military service in 1984, Claudio was not sure what to do with his life so he worked at his brother-in-law's gelato shop. In the nineties, Claudio departed from his brother-in-law's shop to set up his own gelato supply company – with a vision to produce better products for gelato shops. Yet due to lack of foresight, Claudio spent his entire budget on setting up a *laboratorio* rather than buying the ingredients.

"Premixed syrups are the most economic solution in a company's interest, and you know why?" he says. "Because labor is very expensive, and our work is very slow. Think about raw ingredients like pistachios. You have to find them, select them, and shell the pistachios. Then you have to toast them, cool them, and mince them very slowly in order not to warm the oil too much. It's a very long process. So opening a jar of shelled pistachios is a lot easier. Use raw ingredients if you have the passion to do it. And I have a lot of fun doing it, even if I have been doing this for thirty years."

He has the passion for raw ingredients. Claudio scrapped his idea of a gelato supply company and opened a gelato shop in 2003. He laments about the Italian's discomfort with the unknown and hesitation with unusual flavors. Claudio wants to open a shop in France and the United States where he believes gelato lovers are open to new ideas. He would make provocative gelato. "Or use very large cones!" he says. "I was lucky, and [Il Gelato] attracted more and more customers."

He quiets now, his voice retreating. His shyness overcomes him, and he apologizes for talking so much. Claudio frowns as he remembers shops that didn't work out in Rome—the grand openings with spacious storefronts. Now he wants an intimate shop where friends and family can linger over gelato.

At an Il Gelato in a sleepy neighborhood a few subways stops from the historical center, I sample the sushi *aperitivo*, a Japanese savory plate that Claudio makes for happy hour. In a spoonful, the salmon gelato and cucumber gelato remind me of a sushi roll. Another plate arrives, presenting traditional snacks common to an Italian *aperitivo*—breadsticks, vegetables, cheese, and cured meats—and bowls of gelato. There's the mushroom gelato, a dark woody flavor. The bright orange habanero chili gelato combines crispness and spicyness on my tongue. A lick of the light blue-green Gorgonzola cheese gelato is tangy and creamy. The shop is empty now, and I settle near the window. I roll a slice of prosciutto around cheese and a breadstick, dipping it all in olive oil. Then to wash it down, I take a spoonful of the bell pepper gelato, letting the cold sweetness finish the afternoon.

As a child, Claudio remembers Nerini, a gelato shop near his grandfather's hometown. He would climb a huge step to get inside to have his favorite flavor—gelato mixed with cream, chocolate, and buttermilk. Even today, as an adult, the struggle to climb the step remains. Yet, he struggles to recreate the flavor to match the childhood memory. On a recent visit, the gelato is too sweet. Then on another visit, the gelato lacks the expected sweetness. Perhaps it's the eggs, he muses, the cream, or the butter. "I have this flavor right here in my head, the taste, the aroma, and now I am always trying to repeat that specific wonderful taste," Claudio says. "My work is love and hate."

I ask to take a photo, and he politely declines. "I prefer the memories," he says.

Fior di Luna

Fior di Luna has a mission: make handmade gelato from whole ingredients, even donkey milk. Located in the Trastevere neighborhood, the gelateria serves gelato only in cups, because cones would distract from the taste.

fiordiluna.com

Via della Lungaretta, 96

+39 06 6456 1314

"What is the thing you are seeing right now?" Aldo asks me.

The gelato slides across my tongue. The taste of strawberry bursts with intensity, reminding me of baskets of fresh strawberries at the farmers market. The lemon gelato leaves a sour and sweet taste, like the Meyer lemons in my parents' front yard. The fig gelato reminds me of the fig tree that dropped the ripe fruit all over my grandparents' lawn, leaving a honey-like fragrance of stickiness.

"Our idea is to imagine someone tasting gelato, she should close her eyes and see the image of what she's eating. She should not be seeing a cake or delicatessen with that particular flavor. Rather she must *experience* the precise flavor and the *thing* that brings that flavor—the direct experience of the raw ingredient."

Aldo and Fabio Pasquarella are brothers and owners of Fior di Luna, a gelateria located in the neighborhood of Trastevere. Tucked along cobblestone walkways, the gelateria is world-renowned for its dedication to quality ingredients. Framed by green vines, the wooden doors open on a tiled space dominated by a display case. Gelato lovers don't need to sit, because once armed with gelato, they meander through the narrow alleys of the neighborhood—a food mecca of Rome's best bakeries, popular delicatessens, and busy restaurants.

Fabio describes a visitor who tasted fig gelato. The visitor told the brothers that he was not eating fig gelato. "No!" the visitor clarified. "I am right there on a tree, *eating* figs!"

"[Our gelato] is a sensory experience, and it ought to bring you to the natural source, the earth, the soil," Aldo says. "We really want the producers of our ingredients to come here and interact with visitors. It means very much to us. We feel that our visitors should know and have the right to know these people. The idea is to create a little community: there's us, there's our visitor, there's our supplier, and together we talk about what we eat and what we produce...we do that together."

Fabio illustrates the idea: "When farmers bring their fruit, they stop for awhile most of the time, if only for ten minutes, and we offer them gelato. They often talk to our visitors."

"And they often choose the gelato with the same fruit they produce!" Aldo says. "So you can see, it all hangs together. It all comes full circle."

Born in Switzerland, the brothers moved with their parents to Italy in 1960. Gelato ran in their veins. Their parents owned a small café that served gelato in Monteverde. Their mother worked in a gelato factory, and Aldo would visit to watch the process. Factory employees offered Aldo gelato. "I think that was my imprinting," he says and laughs.

Not intending to work in the food business, the brothers studied science at university. Aldo studied aeronautical engineering, and Fabio studied mathematics and pharmaceutical sciences. When Aldo was writing his thesis, tragedy struck in the family. Their father passed away, and they decided to take a different path in life. Rather than focusing on their studies, the two focused their life on working in the family cafe.

Their education provided the framework to approach gelato scientifically—specifically around the chemistry required to "respect the raw ingredient" while maintaining the structure of the sweet dessert. After meeting a gelato maker from Tuscany, the brothers became inspired. Fabio and Aldo studied food texts at the Roman National Library, even from 18th century work to understand the components of gelato. A few years later, they opened their *laboratorio* in Monteverde near their parents' cafe.

"The more [ingredients] you remove, the harder it is to make the gelato, especially when it is so common to use any type of additives to

get the final outcome," Aldo says. Because of the sugar used, the gelato can only last one day. Fabio mentions a large Italian chain would see that as a "flow problem" or defect, but for Fior di Luna, it's a "great virtue." In 1994, the brothers worked hard to make their gelato certified organic—the first gelato of its kind in Italy. They studied with Nico Valerio, a well-known Italian food writer, to understand the balance of foods. Like the Hippocrates quote says, Nico Valerio's philosophy is: *Let food be thy medicine and medicine be thy food.* The gelato from Fior di Luna is progress, even though the brothers gave up organic certification due to demanding restrictions. "But this does not mean that we are using chemical products," Fabio emphasizes.

For them, it's important to maintain tradition and culture. Throughout Rome, I strolled by shops emblazoned with the word "artisanal." Yet those "artisanal" shops carried *poufo* gelato, a blue-colored gelato named after the cartoon The Smurfs. The gelato is like bubble gum ice cream found in the United States—cloyingly sweet and artificial. Other shops pile gelato in mountains decorated with swishes of black and magenta syrups. The brothers frown at that description. "We are worried that more [gelaterias] think they deserve to be called artisans, when it's clearly not the case," Aldo says. "We do not have any legislation. So everyone can use it, even ones who do not whip and stir ingredients, just take pre-existing gelato and put ingredients inside."

In 2003, they met an artisanal gelato maker in the Roman neighborhood of Trastevere. He was looking to sell his business. Sensing an opportunity, the brothers purchased the location and opened Fior di Luna. As they tell me the story, we gaze at the pedestrian walkway outside. Aldo tells us that it's over 200 years old, an ancient Roman road. "You can trace a line that goes from Palatine Hill to Porta Aurelia, and our place - our street - intercepts this path. The foundation of our building originates from an ancient Roman house. This part dates back to 300 A.D., while the front dates back to 1600. So, people have been living and hanging around here for a long time."

Tradition touches their choice of ingredients. When a donkey milk producer from Basilicata contacted the brothers, they were intrigued, because donkey milk is an Italian tradition—Romans once bathed in donkey milk, and Pope Francis revealed that he drank donkey milk as an infant. The brothers experimented and discovered that since donkey

milk has no fat, it allows the pure flavors in their gelato to shine instead of competing against the milk and cream. Today, donkey milk gelato is offered seasonally.

The brothers continue to innovate, and the popularity of the shop spreads through word of mouth. American visitors are beloved by the brothers, because they enjoy understanding the rationale behind their process. Years ago, the brothers traveled to the San Francisco Bay Area and met Alice Waters, restaurant owner of Chez Panisse and a pioneer in the Slow Food movement. Slow Food, by definition, is the cooking philosophy to use only locally grown, seasonal ingredients. She invited the two to make gelato as a celebration of the restaurant's 30th anniversary.

Both brothers wear wire glasses. Fabio wears a t-shirt printed with Snoopy wearing sunglasses and the words "Joe Cool." Aldo, older by nine years, wears a t-shirt from Rodial, a food distributor. They split the work in half and work everyday from 8 in the morning to 8 in the evening. As they tell the story in rapid Italian, often over each other, they point out their machines—the gleaming pasteurizer and freezer.

The shop's namesake *Fior di Luna* originates from the name given to the Childlike Empress in Michael Ende's *The Neverending Story*. In English, the name is "Moon Child". But the literal translation from Italian is "Flower of the Moon."

"Nobody has ever asked that question," Fabio says with a laugh.

On their website, updated since we last spoke, it reads that their namesake reflects the "rapport, friendship, and trust" that they need to achieve their mission of authentic gelato.

Gelateria di Gracchi

Gelateria Gracchi, located near the Vatican, is named for the street where it is a local favorite. The owner, a former musician, delights in creating happiness for his customers using whole fruit and chocolate in gelato made fresh daily.

gelateriadeigracchi.it

Via dei Gracchi, 272

+39 06 321 6668

"I used to play music," Alberto Manassei says and chuckles. "Will you buy me an American guitar?"

With the love of music running through his veins, Alberto seeks gelato that makes people smile and stop for a moment the way he once did with a guitar. Gelateria Gracchi, located near the Vatican, is named for its street, Via dei Gracchi. The gelateria is a local favorite, a secret from the tourists. Italian locals were stunned that I discovered it. Located in the beloved neighborhood of Prati, people from the neighborhood sing praise even across the Atlantic Ocean—an ice cream maker in New York handwrote "Gracchi" in my notebook to make sure that I visited. Alberto, the owner of the gelateria, delights in creating happiness for his customers, using whole fruit and chocolate in gelato made fresh daily.

As a young man, Alberto loved music, playing guitar and bass. He played in what he describes as the worst clubs—I imagine rooms with sticky floors and audience members' short attention spans. In between gigs, Alberto repaired instruments. One day, his brother asked for support for a new gelateria, and soon, Alberto reached an impasse on his life. "My sense of taste is better than my sense of hearing," he says.

Thus began Gelateria Gracchi. His brother learned to make gelato from paste, the industrialized way. The Italian way of making gelato— from scratch—had been pushed aside in many gelaterias. Using syrups and powders allowed gelaterias to make gelato faster and cheaper. "But I wasn't happy with that kind of gelato at all," Alberto recalls. "Why can't I just have good gelato? Made with real ingredients?"

When my colleague and I arrive, we are ushered into the kitchen, better known in Italy as the laboratorio. "Let me show you something," Alberto says and holds out a bowl of strawberries. "Look at this. This makes my strawberry gelato."

The strawberries are bright red, and the sweet fragrance punctuates the air. On the door of the laboratorio, a handwritten signs reads *la porta va tenuta chiusa*: the door must be kept closed. But this is not to keep customers out. Large windows, like that of a home kitchen, invite customers to peek into the magic world of gelato. A woman wearing a white apron works through a bin of strawberries. With a flick of her gloved hand, the strawberry is hulled and dropped into a smaller bin. The woman smiles a toothy grin as Alberto emphasizes the quality of the fruit to us. Two partially grated lemons lie on a pile of apples and bananas.

Fruit gelato appears during its respective season—a challenge for Alberto in the early days, not because the fruit was scarce, but because customers whined that flavors were not year-round. After the second year, Alberto almost closed the gelateria due to the complaints. Customers moaned strawberry gelato was not bright pink and the pistachio was a pale green unlike the gelato at popular gelaterias. "It's not real," the customers said. "You're lying."

But those unusual colors at Gelateria Gracchi reflect the natural origin of the ingredients. Alberto persevered and maintained his integrity, growing Gelateria Gracchi into a local destination by attracting customers who cared about natural flavors. One of his first flavors, pistachio, represents his work. Sourced from the Bronte region in Sicily, Alberto claims that his is the first gelateria in the area to use those prized pistachios.

Alberto wears an aqua polo shirt and wears a small beard. Students from nearby universities visit and ask him questions about gelato. Alberto basks in sharing his knowledge. Born close to Milan, he embodies the typical Italian urban attitude—he tells it as it is. His interest in returning food to its natural roots came from his parents —his father hails from the classic hilltop town of Umbria and mother grew

up in the Salento region, literally the heel of the boot. Alberto spent sixteen years on the island of Sardinia where he hunted for mushrooms and dabbled in gelato making. As a child and even as a younger man, Alberto was concerned about the importance of many issues in culture and arts. Food, to him, is a perfect starting place. "We can go back to the culture of gelato," Alberto says. "Let's go back to think as we used to do. Why did we lose the culture of making gelato?"

With expertise, Alberto slides multiple varieties into one cup for me. The flavors are exquisite. The cantaloupe is light and crisp, like the melon in a chilled form. The pistachio flavor is snappy and fresh, just like the way Italians say the name: pits-ac-kio. The almond flavor is toasted and mixed with orange zest. There's nougat and milk chocolate. I taste gianduja, a mixture of hazelnut and chocolate—its origin traces back to Northern Italy where limited chocolate was extended by mixing with hazelnut paste. This is no Nutella. The apple-cinnamon gelato recalls an American apple pie. Alberto talks about other past flavors—gelato he created for a wine company, combining peach and Muscat. My colleague tastes the pear and caramel, a reminder of a fruity dessert. Alberto points at the zabaglione, a flavor that reflects a popular Italian dessert of egg yolks, sugar, and sweet wine. The egg yolks leave a rich, satisfying taste, and the sweet wine lifts the flavor to a bitter, but sweet finish. "I love making old-style dessert into gelato," he says. "We are in the country with incredible flavors because of the ingredients that can grow here. I use them."

It's still early in the day. Customers trickle into the gelateria. Stacked seven high, white boxes carrying cones lie ready. Spades with colored handles—blue, white, yellow—wait to scoop gelato. A metal lid in the laboratorio clatters. The woman finishes hulling the strawberries and comes to scoop the gelato for the early customers. She reaches for cups behind her, stacks filling the entire wall. Coins clatter into a jar. A machine beeps. Alberto's cousin enters, younger than Alberto and wearing a gray sweatshirt. Cars honk outside as traffic builds. Buses usher tourists to the Vatican. Several blocks away, lines guide visitors into the Vatican to peer upward at St. Peter's Basilica. They wind around the gardens and check off an item on the bucket list. They may go to their next destination by cab or subway, never once stepping on Via dei Gracchi and oblivious to the existence of Gelateria Gracchi, sitting unassuming on a typical Roman street.

Alberto leans toward me and says, "Next time you come, you have to bring a guitar."

I laugh and ask, "Do you still play?"

"Yes, I still play. Badly. But I still do."

Raspberry Lemon Sorbet

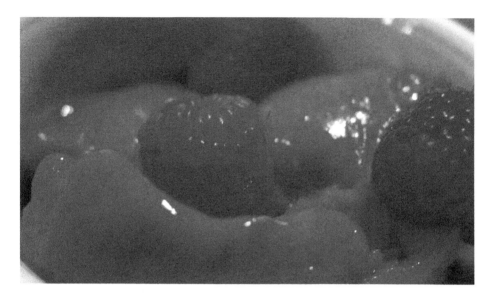

16 ounces of fresh raspberries,
    divided

2 whole lemons (medium to
    large lemons)

2/3 cup of powdered sugar (if
    using granulated sugar, grind
    for about 10 seconds in a
    blender before adding)

Cut one whole lemon into small ½ inch pieces including the peel. Remove all seeds. Add lemon pieces to a blender. Add only the juice of the juice of the second lemon. Blend until a thick puree forms. Small bits of the lemon skin (like fresh zest) will be visible.

Add the raspberries in small batches so that the mixture is blended uniformly. Reserve about 3 ounces of raspberries to use as a topping.

Puree the mixture again. Add more sugar to taste.

For best results, chill the mixture for a few hours, although the mixture can be churned immediately if at room temperature or cooler. Scrape mixture into a pre-frozen ice-cream-maker bowl and churn according to manufacturer's instructions.

The sorbet is best served immediately. To store, scoop raspberry lemon sorbet into an empty resealable container. Freeze up to a month. To serve, let stand at room temperature until slightly softened, about 10 minutes. Serve with raspberries on top.

Sicily: Finding the origin of ice cream on a Southern Italian island

"Sicily is wild," a friend tells me in San Francisco. "But it's wonderful."

By the time I reach Sicily—the final destination in Italy—my enthusiasm for learning about gelato has decreased to a slow drip. Every Italian I meet across the world insists that ice cream was invented in their country, specifically in Sicily, a Mediterranean island at the foot of the mainland. Located strategically along ancient trade routes, its history is tumultuous, fueled by warring feuds and nationalism. It

was here, according to the Greeks and Romans, where Zeus, the ruler of the Olympian gods, buried the fearsome monster Typhon, the cause of Mt. Etna's volcanic eruptions. The calm blue sea contrasts with the active volcano, which rises over 10,000 feet. This island is the home of the Mafia and *The Godfather*.

But I know Sicily as *the* place for food. Not just food to satiate appetites after work. It is the food of love, the food of community, and the food of life. This was where Elizabeth Gilbert ate the best pasta in her life in *Eat, Pray, Love*; where Italian-Americans grandmothers longed for kitchens of the Old World.

I have spent four weeks in Italy learning about gelato. Many gelaterias have adopted a low-cost commercialized method. They flavor their gelato with syrups from "Big Gelato." Gelato from whole, raw foods are rare. Sure, there are the experimental young chefs in Rome—but they are unseen by mainstream Italian culture. I had imagined a grandmother stirring a batch of gelato with a wooden paddle, and a grandfather smiling while he cracked eggs and sliced fresh lemons. But families are no longer the heart of the operation. Instead, I see mounds of gelato decorated with crisscrossed chocolate syrups and dark red jam. True, my eyes are beguiled. Yet when the spoon meets my tongue, all I taste is a powdery substance with a sharp finish.

I had believed that gelato creation was a craft.

I take a one-hour flight from the Italian mainland to Palermo, the capital city located on the west side. Specks of green islands peek through the blue Mediterranean Sea. The towns grow in size until red-roofed houses start piling up on the hills. When I stumble out of the airport, the hot air grabs me in a fist. I see the city's symbol painted everywhere: a peaceful woman's face, sprouting angelic wings, and a circle of legs bent at the knee. I hike through the graffiti-ridden buildings, still broken from wars in the last century. Inside a palace, crooked strips of white tape dance across walls of painted figures.

Churches dot the island. They contain a rare combination—the walls are full of paintings of everyday pastoral life, alongside flowing, golden Islamic script, and renditions of Jesus surrounded by angels. Multiple languages flow through Sicily—hints of a time when empires fought over this piece of land. Centuries-old towns perch on hilltops as they did in an era where incoming warships were a constant threat. Today, new developments grow along the coast. Locals tell me that I'll see the best sunsets in the world.

"Everyone must get two kilos before they leave Sicily," my guide, a rotund man, says to me in broken English. "You must!"

I raise my eyebrows, confused. Get two kilos? I immediately visualize a large plastic baggie being pushed upon me. Can I say no? Noticing my reaction, the rotund man laughs and rubs his belly, "Two kilos from eating!"

Hearing of my quest to learn about ice cream, he sweeps me from shop to shop. I dip pieces of brioche into the cloyingly sweet gelato. The vanilla is pleasing, but I can barely stand the strawberry flavor.

We climb up and around broken pavement and stop in front of Teatro Massimo, Palermo's biggest cultural landmark. A thin, older

man stands underneath a large yellow sign with red painted script reading "Grattatella all'Antica." Old-fashioned shaved ice. Not gelato. He smiles broadly and wears a striped red cap. A blue apron with the city's symbol flaps as he moves swiftly between the ice and sugar. He is out here with his cart every day during the warm months.

The syrups are freshly made that morning. The lemon *grattatella* twists in sweet sourness on my tongue, and the orange *grattatella* adds a juicy layer. The almond *grattatella* surprises me—the ground almonds add a deep nutty flavor while cooled by ice. The rainbow of syrups dazzles customers as they imagine mixing berries and kiwi. The older man moves two large metal scrapers back and forth across a large, flat block of ice, and scoops the small chunks into a plastic cup. A colleague selects a bottle of syrup and pours it all over the ice.

"Sugar?" he asks. Receiving an affirmation, he nods to the colleague.

Two heaping spoonfuls of sugar drop into the cup. To finish, two plastic straws and a plastic spoon are thrust into the concoction. I sip the grandiose treat, relishing the icy-cool respite from the humidity.

I ask the older man why he chooses to sell *grattatella*. Before he answers, the rotund man shakes his head and waves at me, saying, "Because it makes money!"

The older man smiles and says, "Because it's what my father-in-law did to help his poor family in the 1950s. When he died, he told me, 'You must carry on the tradition.'"

The *grattatella* is sweet and refreshing, but it's not what I was craving. I want fruit to be highlighted as the main ingredient rather than ice.

Four days later, I take a break from gelato. I am at a loss now with no English interpreter, and I head out to a village to find something to eat. I stop at a market stall, showcasing boxes of fresh fruits. It reminds me of my weekend habit, visiting farmers markets and concocting dishes from my spoils. Here, I find peaches, strawberries, pears, apricots, melons, and plums. I spot the orange loquats in a box marked *nespoles*, 2.50 Euros. As I finger them, a man approaches me, shuffling quickly on a cane. "You like those?" he says in English, noting my non-Sicilian features. "Most foreigners don't know those *nespoles*."

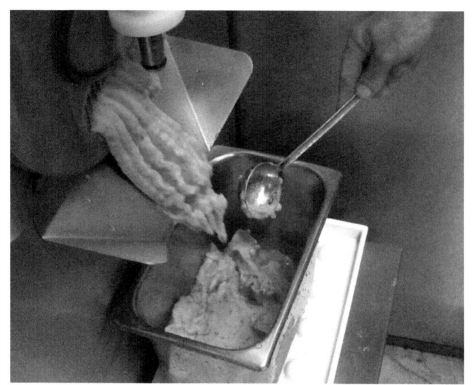

"My parents used to have a tree like this," I say. "But it stopped bearing fruit. I am so excited to see them here."

"Oh, you're an American?" he smiles. "I lived there for many years, but I came back here."

"Why Sicily?" I ask.

"It's the best place to be. My favorite weather is here. My family is here. My friends are here. Everything is here."

Next, I travel to Giarre on the east coast. I stay on a farm, twenty-five miles from the volcanic peak of Mt. Etna. The farm grows citrus and vegetables year-round, in soil fertile from volcanic deposits. I have landed in an ancient region where the wealthy sent their servants to fetch snow to be flavored with fruit and wine.

Salvo, my host and the owner of the farm, picks me up from the train station. "Are you *fame*? *Come si dice in inglese fame*?" How do you say in English *fame*?

"Hungry," I offer. "Yes, I am!"

"Okay, granita!" he twists his wheel to the left.

Salvo swings the car around the tight curves on our way to a bakery at the downtown traffic circle. He wears a t-shirt and shorts. His hair is dark, and his voice is light and fiery.

La Rotonda is non-descript. Customers sit on the front patio shielded with large colorful plastic sheets. They sip finger-sized ceramic mugs of coffee and nibble on pastries. Glasses full of bright slush catch my eye. Granita.

Granita is unlike gelato. It is mostly made out fruit, sugar, and water,—landing between a sorbet and shaved ice. In Giarre, the granita is smooth, unlike its coarser cousins in the western part of the island.

Wherever they are located, granita lovers tear a piece of brioche and dip it into granita, often topped with *panna* or whipped cream. Over time, the color lightens as the granita and *panna* mixes—the deep purple *gelsi* or mulberry becomes a pale purple.

"Ice cream lover? That's a job?" Salvo smiles, examining my business card where "Ice Cream Lover" appears after "Writer" and "Traveler". "Good, but you are in the land of granita!"

We return the next day with Salvo's young children excited in the backseat.

"What is your favorite flavor?" I ask Salvo's son.

Shyly in perfect English, he says, "Chocolate."

"They love chocolate," Salvo says.

Inside the shop, Sebastiano the granita maker presents us a large bucket of bright red strawberries. He wears a white paper hat, like those found at an American old-fashioned ice cream parlor. The paper hat just barely covers his receding hairline. When Sebastiano grins, he exudes the warmth of a grandfather. Salvo and Sebastiano speak in a Sicilian dialect, sounding like muddled Spanish to my American ears. In a smaller basket, he displays strawberries the size of bracelet charms. They originate in the nearby town of Maletto. I ask what these are. "Literally, strawberry of the forest," he says. "It's my secret to great strawberry granita."

The strawberries are mashed together into thick puree in a large white bucket with a sprout. He pours the fruit puree and sugar into a silver machine.

As the machine hums, I ask Sebastiano how long he has been making granita. A grin grows across his face, "Ever since I was born!"

In five minutes, the churned mixture of fruit and sugar is ready. Salvo's kids hungrily grab for the granita. The younger one, a shy boy of six years old, suddenly becomes animated, jostling with his older sister. "He only likes chocolate," Salvo says. "But when there's fresh granita here, he can't help it!"

As we get into the car, Salvo says, "My kids love you for asking about the granita. It's their best memory of the summer. Thank you."

Twenty hours before I return to San Francisco, I eat my last dinner while listening to a dubbed American TV show, and watching Salvo's other guests chat in German, Italian, and Spanish. The sky now slowly darkens around Mt. Etna while the sun makes it way down to the sea. Outside, the air is humid, but it's cool in the grand dining space. Salvo ambles from table to table checking on each guest. His daughter whisks away my empty plate and returns proudly with a white bowl of strawberry granita—the granita that we made just five hours ago.

I dig a spoon into the small mound and taste the granita. I close my eyes and smile. The two types of strawberries meld together into a burst of tart sweetness, melting my restrained frustration after the long trip. At a nearby table, Salvo notices and says, "Granita is best the day it is made. Tomorrow, it will be ice."

Epilogue

Simply put, I love ice cream in a bowl, in a cone, from a tub, and most of all, on my tongue. But why travel so far from home to find it? It started on my first morning in Bangkok in February 2009.

Jet-lagged and sleep-deprived, I sat up at 6 AM. Outside, the haze of the Bangkok skyline appeared outside the ninth-floor hotel window. Exhaustion tore at my eyes, demanding sleep that wouldn't come. For the next two weeks, I would be traveling with eleven people—classmates, friends, friends of friends, significant others. My boyfriend had backed out of the trip two months earlier, worried about unemployment during the recession. I had pushed aside my disappointment and started planning. Hotels! Airplane tickets! Ladyboy shows! Kickboxing! Ancient ruins! Cooking classes! On the flight over, I studied guidebooks and practiced Thai words—Sawatdee for hello and Khob Khun for thank you.

But now I couldn't sleep, and my mind spun. I tossed and turned in bed. Alone. Tired. Angsty. I don't like beaches. I felt abandoned. What if I didn't like the group activities? Why did I agree to this travel destination—an idyllic movie setting for tourists who make bad decisions? Why didn't I stay home and save money? I needed to get out of this hotel room.

"I'll be back," I mumbled to a sleeping friend. "I am going to take a walk."

Outside, the heat rose, a stark contrast to the chilly mornings of San Francisco. Thai script in red spray paint filled a wall, like blood splatters. Through windows, I heard pots and pans clattering as the day's cooking commenced. Young students in uniform gossiped as if I wasn't present. Above, construction workers stomped through twenty-floor building skeletons. A banner in English declared, "We build what you dream." Stopping on an overpass, I stared at the strange cityscape—familiar golden arches poking through concrete buildings, shacks, and power lines.

I passed a colorful open-air market, bustling with morning activity. Small scales lay ready for weighing. Garlands of jasmine flowers graced the rows of stands, punctuating the air with their scent. Housewives bartered. Locals gawked with broken teeth. I dragged my feet, wondering about what I had gotten myself into. All I saw were endless rows of things that I didn't want to eat, unfamiliar Thai faces, a foreign land.

Then suddenly, there it was. A metal cart rolled down the road, ringing seductive bells. It glistened in the sun, and I recognized a symbol—a circle on top of a triangle. Ice cream. My eyes widened, and I had to have it.

Just the previous week, I had rushed downtown to the travel clinic.

A woman with thick '80s-style glasses sat me down and dispensed advice. "Only eat food that is cooked in front of you and make sure it is hot," she said.

"Okay," I said, agreeing to her common sense.

"Do not eat cold foods," she said and wagged her finger. "You don't want traveler's diarrhea."

Walking toward the metal box with wheels in Bangkok, I hesitated, remembering the warnings. But then the ice cream man smiled. I smiled back and gestured wildly to the picture of ice cream. "One?" I said as I held up a finger.

As I dug out cash, he placed three scoops on a small cone and handed it to me. I nodded and took a lick, while grasping for the only Thai word I knew. Bowing my head, I said, "Aroy!" It's delicious.

The man chuckled and returned his wrinkled hands to ringing the bells on his cart. Years later, I don't remember the flavors he gave me. Corn? Mango? Dragon fruit? Guava? What I do remember was the feeling of nostalgia—being six years old and stealing a lick from my sister's cone, a preteen receiving a bowl of vanilla ice cream after one of my parents' greasy homemade meals, a college student swallowing ice cream to wash away heartbreaks. As I finished the cone, my heart felt optimistic. My steps were lighter, and I smiled with the locals. I purchased a jasmine garland. I paid a woman to trim my hair. I tasted the broth of spicy noodle soup at a stall. I admired the graffiti that turned rusty nails and peeling paint into smiles. I sampled coconut pancakes. Even better, this ice cream lover avoided food poisoning.

"An ice cream travel guide!" a friend exclaimed when I described my love of finding ice cream when traveling.

It was 2012. I rejected the idea that some considered ice cream "childish." After all, I spent my early twenties convincing friends with cars to drive to far-flung countryside ice cream shops. My twenty-ninth birthday was a walking tour where I led unsuspecting friends to multiple ice cream shops in a "sundae-hopping" adventure. Then my thirtieth was a "happy hour" at a local ice cream parlor, complete with customized soda fountain drinks and ice cream sundaes. My thirty-first I celebrated by creating thirty-one ice cream flavors in one year. And, of course, there was that moment in Bangkok.

I smiled doubtfully at my friend, but the idea crystallized in my mind. I wanted to know whether ice cream was distinct across the world. How did ice cream differ in methods and approach? How do people think about ice cream in each country? What stories do people tell about ice cream? Was there a secret? Why do people like ice cream? Is it different everywhere?

Ice cream means the same to all ice cream lovers. Regardless of language—whether it was in Chinese, Tagalog, or Turkish. When I was in Buenos Aires in Argentina, a forty-something lawyer gleefully led me from ice cream shop to ice cream shop. In New York City, a foodie friend in his late twenties sent me a list of shops that I *must* visit. One shop owner said, "People do not come to an ice cream shop because they want to stay unhappy. They come for rewards and delights. They come because it's a cheap way to have fun. It's a place for a community for all ages."

Halfway across the world as I wandered through Italy, it struck me that I wasn't trying to just learn about ice cream. Rather with my own search for happiness, I wanted to understand how happiness can be achieved through something tangible. Prior to the beginning of the book, I struggled with the meaning of my life, my family, and my career. I was in crisis. A dark shadow fell over me and even with loved ones around me, I couldn't pick myself up. The only thing that I could do was grasp something physical—something that reminded me of the good times. Ice cream is simple and sweet, and I found that alluring. I had decided that the answer to happiness had to be out there. After all, ice cream is beloved around the world. Where does that happiness come from?

You would think that I had some groundbreaking answer. Yet what I discovered is that ice cream is all about community and simplicity.

Ice cream is about childhood. As adults, when we look back in childhood, we recall happy moments with family (for better or worse) and sweet indulgence. Ice cream shops don't forget this. A shop in Los Angeles depicts a toddler holding a cone in its logo. In Istanbul, children's drawings of ice cream are posted throughout a shop. Children were present in every ice cream shop I visited. Despite melted chocolate and rainbow sprinkles on their hands, they were grinning. Ice cream is Proustian in its nature, swinging us back to happy memories.

Due to the global exchange of information, ice cream is accessible for all, and the processes to make it are identical. Local ingredients and local palates might differ, but the delicious cool treat at the end of the warm day is the same for all of us.

My final destination in my travels was Ben & Jerry's headquarters in Vermont. By then, several ice cream makers across the world had cited the ice cream manufacturer as their inspiration. Through their colorful factory and their test kitchen, I discover that ice cream is only one part of the equation. The team tells me about the GMO-free ingredients, the annual giveaway of ice cream, providing same-sex benefits for their employees, and sourcing from a bakery that employs people who cannot find work elsewhere. Taking care of their employees and the company's future is one thing. But it's the social mission that carries the glue: Ben & Jerry's started as a small community business and continue to find innovative ways to improve quality of life across the world. It's about giving back.

This is what I really discovered through my journey: the best ice cream is not the ice cream found at far-flung destinations. It's the ice cream that you can share with others. It may be the ice cream at the local ice cream shop—the fancy one or the not-so-fancy one. It may be the ice cream pint (or gallon) that you purchased at the grocery store.

I believed that the world had an answer for me—as I visited ice cream shop after ice cream shop. I found out that it wasn't out there. Like the saying goes, it was at home all along. Ice cream is community. What I discovered is that ice cream around the world is about the people.

Ice cream is "happiness." Or as my sister pointed out, you can't buy happiness, but you can buy ice cream. So let's go get a scoop.

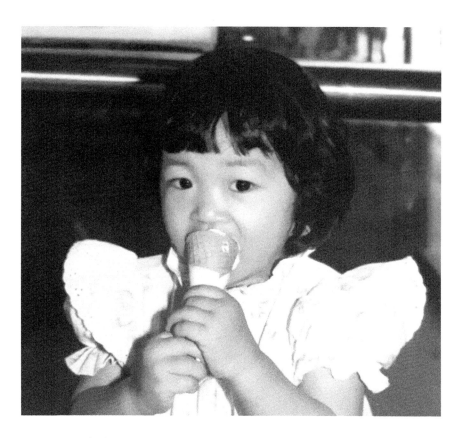

First recorded evidence of the author eating ice cream

Acknowledgements

Thank you to everyone that supported my journey through writing this book. I am humbled by friends and family. Many jumped in to help me with this project. Not everyone loves ice cream as much as I do, and I deeply appreciate everyone's willingness to support me with my vision.

First, I began this book to prove that I could write. Along the way, I learned from fellow writers. Many thanks the writing workshops I took across the nation, especially Jen Cross at Writing Ourselves Whole and Erica Lorraine Scheidt at CCSF's Creative Nonfiction Writing Workshop. And the Writers Grotto classes, especially Steve Almond who probably loves sugar as much I do. A big thank you to the fantastic Eric Simons, a seasoned journalist that gave me tips for interviewing. Of course, I cannot go without thanking Alabama Street Writers Group who saw late drafts as well as my pursuit into writing fiction. They include Chad Schmike, Jenny Schaffer, Jessica Ainsworth, Joy Morgenstern, Mark Pritchard, Maureen Kilkeary, and Merin McDonell. May we continue to meet weekly for years to come!

Second, the Kickstarter campaign served as validation that people were interested in this project. Thanks to Shaun Saperstein, who produced the video and brilliantly transformed my usual slurred speech into a confident voice. Thanks to Will Hsu, who designed the logo and led me through Taiwan with his family. Many props to Jen Ly who offered to take beautiful photos of ice cream and eating it.

Third, all the people I met during my travels were so passionate. I deeply appreciate those who connected me to the ice cream shops, especially in non-English speaking countries. Thank you Valentina at Gelato University and Museum for arranging my visit. Thank you Lindsay, Jay, and Rob at Ben & Jerry's for taking the time to chat. I appreciate hosts who generously shared their time—thank you Stacy in Taipei, Alberto in Palermo, Lisa in Rome. And new friends who were kind enough to share their experiences with me—thank you Paola, Julia, Lisa, Angelica and Fulvio in Italy; thank you Damián and Magdalena in Argentina—you made me feel like a local. Thank you Artemsia for connecting me with gelaterias in Bologna and showing me the right way to have an Italian breakfast. Thank you Jason for taking a break from a busy day in Taipei to talk about ice cream and street food. Thank you Sal and his father, who willingly opened his beautiful home in Sicily to me and served amazing homemade wood fired pizza with fresh ricotta. And major props to Simona, the co-founder of Walks of Italy, a tour group based in Rome. I owe so much to Deniz in Istanbul who willingly interpreted a conversation with an ice cream maker while political demonstrations called for his attention. Thank you for taking a break from the tear gas and fighting for Turkey's intended state of a nation.

Fourth, there are all the Kickstarter backers. Their names are (as they wanted printed): A. Mistry, A. van Zett, Alecky, Alex Darrow, Alison Wong, Anna Saccheri, Anonymous, Armond Netherly, Ben Elgart, Bo Ren, Carolyn Atkins, Chadwyck Montford Bennett Wirtz, Chloe Fan, Chris Ong, Christopher "TaiChE" Tai, Chung-Hay Luk, Cohousing California, Cristal Lim, Cuyler, Dan & Nancy Colachicco, David H. Nguyen, David Mahoney, David Rajan, David Zhen, dawnalee, Delon R. Ferdinand, Derek Jay Steen, Diana To, Dinh Luong, Doreen Ng a.k.a. Little Sis, Eliot, Endre Kodolanyi, Erica Anne Kuntz Romanoski, Esther Leong, Fabian Falconett, Federico Soria, Frances Chou, Guadalupe Albuquerque, Ham Shin, Hari & Eric & Eleanor Simons, Heidi Mato, Huong Le, Ian Li, Ish Harshawat, Izzi & Rozi the ice-cream loving puppies, Jack :), Jagoda Amanda, Jaireh Tecarro, James Tanedo, Jan Holzberg, Janette Fong, Jason Angeles (Founder of Frozen Kuhsterd), Jason T. Wang, Jay Meistrich, Jean Gong, Jeff & Laura Chou, Jenn Chan, Jimmy Kjellström, Jimmy Lin, Joe Leidy, Joe Tullio, John Marsland, JT, Julian Missig, Julie Aranda, Justin Kodama, Kathryn Velikanje, Kavi Harshawat, Kelsey Gallagher, Kendel Shore, Konstantin Voronin and Nicole Lau, Krystle Song, Laura Lu, Laurie Blanton, Lester Lee (who recommended Woodside Creamery in Hockessin), Lillian Chan, Lindsay Metcalfe, Lisa and Danny Dragin (and Andrew and Jacob), Liselle Angeliqe Awwal., Lydia Yeung, Marian Herenius, Mary Austin, Matt Hornyak, Mich Sineath, Mike Sparandara, Noah Solnick, Nuttapol Kamsaeng, Paco the roommate!, Patrici Flores, Paul & Andreina Ng, Paul Petrick, ROdrigo MX, Rachael Ng, Ravi Chandrasekaran, Richie Nocom, Ruqian Gillian Zhou, Ruth Wylie, Ryan Andrews, Sal Ingrilli, Sasha Lee, Scoops Ingram, Scott Kilmartin, Shadia, Shipra Kayan, Simon Linder, Sravana Reddy, Stephanie Au, stephenryanlee, Steve Hillenius, Steve Wang, Sweta M, t, The Phaengdara Potter's, Therese Cornell-Ramoran, Tina Soo Kim, Tinna Ho, Tomomi Imura, Tutti Taygerly, Victor Cheng, Wenchi,

Wendy Chan (who recommended Fior di Luna in Rome), Will Ober, Will Ritter, Yue Xia, YuWei Will Hsu, Zachary Sam Zaiss, and Zichuan Lian..

Fifth, thank you for everyone who helped me make the final product. Thank you Laura Zattra, Martina Puppi, Martina Scarano, and Juan Font for translations from audio. Thank you Diana Stanciulescu for illustrating the maps. Thank you Bethany Andrews and Ani Manjikian for editing the manuscript.

Sixth, thank you to my parents who introduced me to ice cream. They believed that once a child could have solid food, that a child must experience ice cream. To my dad, you taught me not to leave ice cream stains in the living room, but I suppose now I am leaving an ice cream stain on the world.

Seventh, thank you to Chris who never wavered in his belief for this book. Even in the hardest of times when I wanted to give up, you were always there. You are the only other person I know who can eat as much ice cream as me in a day, perhaps even more. Thanks for the final copyedits at the 25th hour. This book is dedicated to you.

Finally, the ice cream makers. You are the core of this book, and all of you have inspired me by your passion and perseverance to your craft. Thank you for letting me share your story.

About the Author

Jennifer Ng is a writer and design consultant living in San Francisco. She writes creative nonfiction and fiction. This is her first book.

Her favorite ice cream flavor changes depending on what is in season in her geographic location. Fruits are the best. Jennifer believes that there is no such flavor as the weirdest flavor. Rather, it is the most unfamiliar taste profile. Prior to this book, she created thirty-one ice cream flavors in the twelve months leading to her thirty-first birthday—some of those recipes appear in this book.

Read more on icecreamtravelguide.com

CPSIA information can be obtained
at www.ICGtesting.com
Printed in the USA
FSOW03n2101090616
21371FS

9 780997 608601